3:14 AND OUT

A Collection of
Vermont Public Radio Commentaries
by
Bill Mares

Bill Mares

Also by Bill Mares

The Marine Machine (1971), *Doubleday*

Passing Brave (1973) with William Polk, *Knopf*

The Golden Ode(1974) with William Polk, *U. Of Chicago Press*

Working Together (1983) with John Simmons, *Knopf*

Real Vermonters Don't Milk Goats, (1983) with Frank Bryan,
New England Press

Making Beer (1984) *Knopf*

Out: The Vermont Secession Book, (1987) with Frank Bryan,
New England Press

Out Of Order (1991) with Frank Bryan, *New England Press*

Fishing with the Presidents (1999) *Stackpole Books*

The Vermont Owner's Manual (2000) with Frank Bryan,
New England Press

Bees Besieged (2005) *A.I.Root Co.*

A Collection of
Vermont Public Radio Commentaries
by
Bill Mares

Published by Wind Ridge Publishing, Inc.
Shelburne, Vermont 05482

3:14 AND OUT
A Collection of Vermont Public Radio Commentaries

Published by Wind Ridge Publishing, Inc.
P.O. Box 752
Shelburne, Vermont 05482

ISBN: 978-1-935922-07-0
Library of Congress: 2011940104

3:14 AND OUT

A Collection of
Vermont Public Radio Commentaries
by Bill Mares

Acknowledgements

Since 1988, Vermont Public Radio has offered a distinctive series in which cross sections of Vermonters are invited to sound off about the human condition. I have been lucky that careers in journalism, politics and teaching, plus lots of travel, provide me with a smorgasbord of interests and experiences that I can draw on for my offerings.

Writing is never easy, but I like this form of short personal essay. To say something coherent in five hundred words means that every word counts—while still trying to find the universal in a subject, to connect my own life to the world around me, and to do so without leaving my thumbprint on the windowpane. When asked to give a speech, Woodrow Wilson once replied, "If you want me to speak for an hour, I can do it tomorrow. If you want me for thirty minutes, give me a week, but if you want only five minutes, I need a month."

In my serial revisions, I am mindful of a quote from William Strunk and E.B. White's classic *The Elements Of Style*. They write, "Omit needless words, omit needless words, omit needless words..." So no matter how fine the grain, there is always more grinding to be done. This is not poetry, after all!

I'll get an idea and try it out on my wife, or one of my running buddies. If it passes that smell test, I send the thought to Betty Smith at VPR headquarters for her green light. I begin by scribbling notes on a yellow pad. Then like a dog with a bone, I gnaw on it for a few days before burying the first draft in the computer. Several days later, I'll dig it up again. I gnaw some more until I can send a clean copy to Betty. If I'm lucky, it will come back with "just a few tweaks." Sometime, she wants major revisions, and we go back and forth three or four times. Further polishing comes by reading the piece aloud. It's amazing how many typos, non-sequiturs, and other grammatical flaws appear in audible speech.

The scene now shifts to the VPR studio where engineers Sam Sanders and Chris Albertine take their shots. Inside their headphones, they have the unfailing ears of the average listener who must understand "at fifty miles an hour." There is always a glitch, a stumble over some alliterative allusion or other phrasing that looked so smooth on paper but was so rough in the mouth. Fortunately, Sam and Chris can make their repairs sentence by sentence. We seldom need to re-tape the entire piece. Rarely do I listen to my own commentaries. I've poured my best into their creation; I don't want to be reminded of the flaws that remain. Besides, it's time to move on to the next one.

To my wife Chris Hadsel, and Mike Martin, a fellow teacher and VPR commentator who both encouraged me to try this format, and to Betty Smith who helped turn the weeds of my thoughts into the garden of this selection, I dedicate this volume.

Foreword

About ten years ago, when about the third person asked me out of the blue whether I knew Bill Mares, I figured I'd better get to know him. Surely if people who knew me thought I'd enjoy his company, they were probably right. And they were.

We share things in common. We're both former secondary school teachers. I used to practice law; he realized law wasn't for him while he was still in law school. He's a journalist and writer by profession, the road I didn't take. I'm a broken down runner and marathoner; he's still at it in his retirement, the lucky guy. I'm an old technical climber and mountaineer; he's a devout fly fisherman and fellow lover of the outdoors. We're both devoted to Vermont.

Above all, we both love books, ideas, current events, good conversation, and good humor. Conversation with Bill is substantive, animated, and fun. Dinner table discussion is invariably wide-ranging, but also focused; Bill seeks clarity, understanding, and resolution—even though it can only be, as Robert Frost said about poetry, "a momentary stay against confusion."

In addition, we're both Vermont Public Radio commentators. Indeed a few years ago, amidst talk of such things at the dinner table, a fleeting, distant look on his face—as if an idea had just come to him—causes me to speculate that my doing VPR commentaries caused him to do the same. VPR's listeners—and now countless readers—are enriched as a result.

These selected essays, originally VPR commentaries intended to be heard, are also great to read. They explore the breadth of subjects that you would expect from such a capacious and energetic mind. Mares brings to his more light-hearted essays an informed thoughtfulness that justifies and enriches our pleasure in reading them, and he brings to the more serious pieces an approachability and charm that comes from his love of learning, teaching, and exploring the world of ideas. He wears his knowledge and intelligence lightly, inviting others along on the journey.

Here, as in his conversation, we find not fiction or fantasy, but an unblinking consideration of the world as it is. Mares subscribes to the great essayist Francis Bacon's belief that, "The contemplation of things as they are, without error or confusion, without substitution or imposture, is in itself a nobler thing than a whole harvest of invention." He reminds us that people are entitled to their opinions, but not to their own facts. And while admonishing us that "feelings are not thoughts and thinking is hard work," he shows us that thinking can also be the source of profound emotion and also great fun.

Mares clearly fits his definition of an intellectual, which he takes from Arthur Schlesinger—"a person at home with ideas." It is a democratic, American definition. Appropriately, his license plate reads "THINK." But he is as much about the celebration of life as he is about cerebration. Like Tennyson's Ulysses, Mares "drinks life to the lees."

There's a muscular warmth to these essays, like the author's firm handshake. They are informed, like their author, by vitality, curiosity, humor, and a humane generosity of spirit.

Mares defines good friends as "people who inspire me, stimulate me, get me out of myself and accept my weaknesses." I like that definition, and that's why Bill Mares is a good friend.

—Peter A. Gilbert
Vermont Humanities Council

And yet it is also true that one can write nothing readable unless one constantly struggles to efface one's own personality. Good prose is like a windowpane.

—George Orwell

Musings from Home

A Hundred Years of This

In the dripping darkness, I settle into my little foxhole of granite field-stones left from a century-old wall. By feel, I move the twigs and leaves and settle onto my hot seat. Rifle over my lap, I treat myself to coffee straight from the Thermos, a handful of gorp, and wait for the dawn.

This small corner of Northeast Kingdom forest and open land is familiar; it's the only place I've ever deer hunted in Vermont. Gradually, through breath-fogged glasses, the gray light begins to reveal mown fields, dark pines, maple saplings, and birch limbs. A quarter mile away the pencil plume of smoke rises from a neighbor's wood stove. My eyes and ears become merry pranksters. A fluttering beech leaf at five feet looks like a deer at fifty yards. Solitary raindrops sound like deer footfalls.

From several directions comes the ragged drum roll of rifle shots to proclaim the opening of deer season. I tense. Deer in the distance must have cousins nearby. I scan the trees and fields until my eyes ache. Then I relax. Face it: no deer will appear. In thirty-four years I've never killed a Vermont deer, even on the highway. I suppose that makes me a poor hunter. Or more charitably, maybe I just don't try hard enough or in the right places.

And bringing home venison isn't really why I'm here; I can rely on more successful friends. I'm here for the memories; the generational communion of hunting that began fifty-five years ago with my father in Texas, where, yes, I did kill a number of deer. Surprisingly, the central Texas hill country where we hunted was very much like Vermont, except that the cattle were Herefords, not Holsteins, the trees were mesquite and live oak, not maple and birch, and the ground was bare.

I was in awe of my father. He was an extremely hard-working chemical engineer who rarely took a vacation. He was a stern taskmaster to himself and a stern father to his sons. A man of few words, he was given to aphorisms that prized silence, such as "The steam that toots the whistle never turns a wheel."

But on hunting and fishing trips he was relaxed and approachable.

I would bring schoolbooks to study; he would bring a stack of chemical journals. In deer camp I learned to drink coffee and make chili. While we played gin rummy for hours, he told about his hunts in Montana with his father, an immigrant from what is now the Czech Republic. We usually went to different stands, but occasionally we would hunt together in patchwork blinds, sharing Hershey bars and licorice sticks, as we scanned the landscape in silence. One morning, in nose-dripping cold, we watched the sunrise in a handful of minutes go from pink to salmon to orange and finally blazing white across of the valley. A wild turkey gobbled in the distance.

"You know," he said, "It would take a hundred years of this to kill you."

Slow But Literate

The historian Arthur Schlesinger once defined an intellectual as a person "at home with ideas." That's a fair definition of the members of our Big Boys Book Club, a men's reading group now beginning its third decade.

Our members have included doctors, lawyers, academics, engineers, and oddballs like me that were brought together by a shared intellectual curiosity and love of reading. "This setting and these people," said member Vince Feeney, "encourage us to tackle books we might not read otherwise."

Once a month we gather at a member's house from 7:30 to 9:00 on a Sunday evening. Fueled by decaf and cookies, we chew over recent fiction, non-fiction, best-sellers, and also-rans. A selection of books from the past year include *"A Short History of Nearly Everything,"* by Bill Bryson, *"The Double Bind,"* by Chris Bohjalian, *"Water for Elephants"* by Sara Gruen, *"The Age of Turbulence"* by Alan Greenspan, *"Dreams from My Father"* by Barack Obama, and *"A Long Way Gone"* by Ishmael Beah.

After a few minutes of chitchat, we are off and talking. These collective ruminations are both relaxed and intense. No one has to talk. No one has to have the last word. No one "leads" the discussion. We find our own line of enquiry and disdain the guided questions that have become common in the Oprah Book Club era. The only rule is that you can't trash the book for the first fifteen minutes of discussion. After that, the pages can become a free-fire zone.

Like barn swallows, members swoop in and out of the discussion depending upon their whims or the strength of their views. The evening becomes a kind of intellectual quilting bee where different minds add strong or muted swatches to the overall pattern. Generally, we stay on target, but sometimes we veer off track to discuss vacations, politics, or families. A few prospective members have found us a bit too eclectic, or not rigorous enough.

Naturally, I feel better if I've read the scheduled book, but sometimes I can't. Yet I go anyway, bulking up on reviews, the cover blurbs and preface—happy to listen to sharp minds at play. We've come to trust the other Big Boys to choose good books and have honest, forthright opinions.

The evening's host gets to choose the new book. After we've exhausted the current volume, like a casino black-jack dealer, he passes around five or six books and gives a few seconds' description. From the ensuing short discussion when members weigh both topic and book, a consensus emerges. Thanks to Bob Rinkema, a retired computer network consultant, we live in cyberspace with our own website. And a Big Boys Athletic Club has entered relay teams in several Vermont City Marathons. Our slogan says it all: "Slow But Literate."

Making Pictures, Not Taking Pictures

The mean streets of Chicago were already littered with the rusty hulks of my first three career choices when I stumbled into photojournalism many years ago. I was swallowed whole by the joy and challenge of shaping my world through a camera lens and compressing three dimensions into two.

I'd never managed drawing beyond stick figures, but with a camera I could paint and sculpt, looking for what the French photographer Henri Cartier-Bresson called "the decisive moment," referring to that "creative fraction of a second when your eye must see a composition or an expression that life itself offers you," and learn to intuit when to click the shutter. It was magic to see by amber light my images rising out of a darkroom tray: the good, the bad, and the woeful. For me, black and white was always more expressive than color, which left little to the imagination.

My chief mentor, and eventually my best man, was an African-American named John Tweedle whose Falstaffian voice I hear today: "Shoot close, crop tight! Make pictures, don't take pictures!" Besides Cartier-Bresson, my heroes were Robert Capa, David Douglas Duncan, Nick Adams, Dorothea Lange, Walker Evans, and Robert Frank. I achieved a measure of success, with several books of photographs and an exhibit at the Art Institute of Chicago.

Then I moved on to other things. But a quote by Francis Bacon, also a favorite of Dorothea Lange, has stayed with me ever since:

"The contemplation of things as they are, without error or confusion, without substitution or imposture, is in itself a nobler thing than a whole harvest of invention."

Bees and the Tunbridge World's Fair

Not too long ago, I joined my friend Mike Palmer of St. Albans for our annual turn in the beekeepers' booth at the Tunbridge World's Fair. Mike is the president and I'm the vice-president of the 220-member Vermont Beekeepers Association. For seven hours, a steady stream of people gaped at bees in our observation hive, sucked up free samples of honey, and occasionally bought some. Over and over they asked variations of the same question: What's happening to the bees? What is this new disease? Are Vermont bees safe?

Mike is a professional beekeeper and I am a hobbyist. We were both pleased that people were so curious about the health of the bees. Alas, in that crowded, noisy hall, we could not give them a quick answer or a single villain. So far, we said, Vermont bees seem to have avoided the massive bee die-offs reported in other parts of the country. Nationally, we now know that there is no single cause for the bee malady dubbed colony collapse disorder.

You have to think of three strands in the investigative puzzle, we told our attentive audience: something old, something new, and a lot in between. First, there is a cyclical element. Significant die-offs have occurred before, going back at least one hundred years. Second, a globalization of pests has brought new viruses and pathogens into bees' lives, as well as our own. Third, and most important, is the increased stress on bees over the last twenty-five years. Now, remember that the importance of bees in the American economy is not in honey production—a measly $200 million annually. It is in pollination for hire, some $15 to $20 billion worth of fruits, vegetables, nuts, and forage crops. But that means hauling bees hundreds and thousands of miles each year. Such long-distance strain comes on top of the unrelenting scourge of Asian varroa mites that arrived in the U.S. in the late 1980s and—rather like the Iraqi insurgency—have become more maligned over time. Other troubles include agricultural pesticides used outside the hives, overuse of chemicals inside the hive to fight the mites, and poor nutrition for the overworked bees.

All these pressures of feedlot beekeeping have weakened the bees' immune systems. When you're healthy and get a cold, we said, you recover quickly; when you're already weak, you can get pneumonia or worse.

Most Vermont beekeepers are hobbyists with just a few hives that we don't move around. This gives bees time to recover their strength over the winter. Of the handful of professionals like Mike, only one moves bees out of state each year.

"So what do we do?" asked our last customer, as we closed up shop at 10 p.m. We walked out into the chill air amid the lingering smells of cigarette smoke, onions, cotton candy, and fried dough. "Well," I said, "just keep buying lots of local honey."

Strike's Over

I wasn't going to watch the Super Bowl this year. Lately, I haven't had much appetite for pseudo-patriotism, even on Ronald Reagan's one hundredth birthday. It's not just that I like gun control laws, or that I think the Constitution is a living document that can change, or that the Health Care law makes sense. It's worse.

Moreover, the thought of Super Bowl Sunday paled in comparison to the events in Cairo, with millions of ordinary people taking the streets to free themselves from tyranny's yoke. This was a real struggle. Having been in Tahir Square a couple of times in the past, those intoxicating demonstrations were easier to relate to. I've never been to a Super Bowl.

That's Super Bowl XLV, by the way. The number is in Roman numerals to remind us that this extravaganza had its roots in the Roman feast of Saturnalia. It's the great American secular holiday, a celebration of excess with its special rituals of foods, parties, and plumage. Apart from the simple question of who's going to win, the chief intellectual diversion is the cleverness of the advertisements. Between two halves of mayhem on the field would come the interminable halftime show with its only potential suspense a "wardrobe malfunction" or a flubbed National Anthem.

And where else to hold such a celebration than in the new $1.5 billion palace, a temple to the ego of Dallas Cowboys' owner Jerry Jones? Yeah, the Dallas Texas Cowboys, America's Team, as they tell the world, with a record this year of six and ten! Well this would be the first Super Bowl without cheerleaders!

Then Sunday afternoon my resolve began to slip. Had the Patriots been there, would I be going through mental moral gymnastics? Maybe I'll just check in to see the score. One of our sons, an avid Steelers fan, was six thousand miles away streaming the game. I owe him some loyalty. I'll just watch a few minutes of the second quarter, with the sound off and a good book on my lap. The score was 14-3 Packers.

Halftime came. The score was now 21-10. Well, twenty-five minutes of dead time. Maybe I should go and see what other people were so revved up. I put on a coat and crossed my snowy Rubicon. In ten minutes I was in sensory overload of three huge TV's, wall-to-wall people, and rivers of Guinness. My defenses against athletic jingoism melted like a snowman in sixty-degree weather.

Despite innumerable replays, breathless clichés from press box and sideline, and some pretty dumb ads, I morphed into a Packer cheese-head—without the ridiculous headgear. I forgot about the endless snowstorms, the 9 percent unemployment, and the chaos in Egypt. I groaned at Pittsburgh's comeback. I pounded the bar at Green Bay's victory, and shook the hand of the anonymous Packer fan next to me. I trudged home happy, but I can promise you if the NFL locks out the players, I won't lose sleep...until maybe next November.

Calm, Quiet, Innocent Recreation

Gingerly, I step and slip down the forty-five-degree slope covered with rain-slick pine needles, down to the boulder-strewn bank of a Northeast Kingdom river. The exact location you'll never learn from me; this is one of my favorite fall fishing spots. I always catch fish here. Ten years ago, I caught a twenty-inch rainbow here. Mist rising from the river blots out the far bank. It's cold and will grow colder, before the sun and my excitement thaw my paws.

In the fall you can fish all day long. You don't have to wait for the evening rise. Hungry fish are storing up food for the winter. I'll be storing up memories. In the fall you've got most of the water to yourselves, especially here. I'm alone with my catches—and my misses.

With a wading stick I three-point my way across slippery rocks out into the river. To my ears, manifold water sounds blend into a streamside string quartet of violins, cellos and a viola. I pay out the line with the Zug Bug fly I attached last night. Unlike the early season, this is not a time for dry flies, which are cast to rising fish. I'm fishing blind as it were, hoping for a strike. This is pocket water, where behind each submerged boulder can lurk a lunker or lesser fish. Or so I believe.

I begin casting short and long, across and down, letting the fly drift over those boulders. After ten casts, I change flies. After another ten, I change again. The far shore comes into view. A flock of mergansers flies overhead. The elements pull me in three directions at once. The river pressing against my waders pushes me downstream. A wind blows up-stream into my face. Above, starch-white clouds scud across a blue-denim sky.

Suddenly, 220 volts without the pain shoot through the line and up my arm. A silvery fish cartwheels in the air like a circus acrobat. I raise the rod to keep the tension and pray the fish is good and truly hooked. It races down-stream pulling out fifty feet of line. It jumps again. How can a one-pound fish shake my timbers so?

After two minutes of zigzagging, the fish tires, and with rod held high I maneuver it closer, closer until I slip the net under the squirmy green-backed trout. Goodness, what a fish! This shimmering, flapping, kaleidoscope before my eyes mimics all the fall colors around me, from river to trees to sky. I carefully release the hook and gently return the fish to the water. Two hours later, I scramble up the bank, six fish in my creel of memories and one in my vest, for dinner.

As Izaak Walton, the St. Francis of fly-fishing, wrote almost four hundred years ago, "We may say of angling, as Dr. Boteler said of strawberries, doubtless God could have made a better berry, but doubtless God never did; and so, if I might be judge, God never did make a more calm, quiet, innocent recreation than angling."

Hurricane Season

Hurricanes were as much a part of the life and lore of my Texas Gulf Coast childhood as tropical heat, poisonous snakes, and mosquitoes. Our house was about twenty miles inland from Galveston, but only eight feet above sea level. We lived on Dickinson Bayou, a tidal stream which flowed into Galveston Bay.

Those were the days when all hurricanes had female names. "Hell hath no fury like a woman scorned," was my literary mother's dry explanation. The great Galveston hurricane of 1900, so well described in Eric Larsen's book "Isaac's Storm," was still a vivid memory for people in our town. Some of them lost relatives in what has regularly been listed as the greatest natural disaster in U.S. history. It killed over six thousand people and the city never really recovered.

I was reminded of the times we swam on the Galveston beaches beneath the fifteen-foot barrier that was built after that storm—and of my father's explanation of how the waters had inundated the unprotected city—as I watched TV film of Gulf waters crashing over the Galveston seawall during Ike's assault.

For us kids, hurricanes were more adventures than dangers. Our parents had to decide when to board up the windows, what to stockpile—batteries, canned food, candles, fresh water—as well as if and when to leave for the higher ground. We prepared to manage for days without power or school, and with lots of rain. We were spared the tragedy and gross incompetence of Katrina, and the massive evacuations of Gustav and Ike. But we had a few close calls.

In one hurricane the water rose to our back step and brought lots of snakes out of their holes, although not as many as terrified the Louisiana city of Cameron during Hurricane Audrey in 1957, when snakes and people fled to the same trees. During Hurricane Carla in September 1961, I joined a rag-tag band of National Guardsmen, cops, and other volunteers to drive amphibious vehicles called Ducks into the teeth of the gale to rescue people in the low-lying areas of Galveston. One thing I learned was that it's actually easier to withstand one hundred-mile-per hour winds if you're waist-deep in water.

In the early 1980s, another hurricane (I don't remember the name) passed over our small town. Afterwards, my mother called to say she was safe, but her voice broke when she described the yard littered with over thirty broken and up-rooted trees. "Can you come down and help clean this up?" she asked. "Sure," I said. And so, at my wife's suggestion, I packed up my Jonsered chain saw sharpening file, gloves, helmet, and ear plugs and headed South, attracting a certain measure of curiosity at the baggage carousel in Houston, but no arrest. For four days, in that sticky September heat, I sweated, swore, and cut my way through toppled mimosa, oleanders, cedars, oaks, and pines. On the third day, the power came back on. One of its first blessings was a cold beer.

It Takes More than Food

Ben Runyan says he volunteers at the Chittenden Emergency Food Shelf because, "I needed a more socially-responsible way to spend my free time." Sarah Heim says simply "fighting hunger is a shared community responsibility, and everyone can play a part." Mary Ellen Mannock volunteers to be a part of the larger community. I volunteer there once a week because my religion calls me to help distribute the loaves and the fishes.

In my shift, I do whatever I'm told: stack cans of food, clean out produce bins, unload trucks, direct traffic, grind coffee, bag beans. I crawl around the shelves like a monkey, or load the dumpster with cardboard, or sweep the floor. There is some heavy lifting, but it's not onerous.

I enjoy the people. I can joke with Mike Farmer, the cook, Kevin Glasglow, the warehouse manager, or his assistant V.J. Brkovic. It has an international component where, besides English, you can hear Russian, Somali, French, Swahili, Kirundi, Spanish, Mai Mai, Vietnamese, and Nepalese.

Last week, I chatted briefly with Rob Meehan, the busy director, about some of his efforts to expand the scope and mission of the Food Shelf. In these darkening economic times when more and more people are asking for help, the food shelf stands at the crossroads of poverty and social services, reflecting trends occurring across the country.

Rob said, "This is a place to distribute food to the needy. But we want to do more to help break the cycle of poverty. Our goal is to cultivate opportunities for people who are part of our community." For example, last summer Ben Runyan helped spearhead a community garden in the Intervale so that fresh vegetables could become part of the monthly food allotments. The food shelf is also starting a culinary training program that will prepare clients to be ready for entry-level jobs at Sodexho food services at the University of Vermont.

"What else do you need?" I asked.

"We can always use more volunteers," he said.

A light went on in my head. What if groups that ask members to donate a can of non-perishable food also ask their members to give one hour of volunteer service? As a member of the Green Mountain Athletic Association (GMAA), I knew that the running club sponsors an annual Thanksgiving Day race called the Turkey Trot, in which they ask entrants to donate food to the Food Shelf. What about tapping them?

So I wrote to the GMAA officers asking for its support for this idea. They wrote back almost immediately to say yes, they would be happy to place signs and distribute flyers at the Turkey Trot encouraging people to volunteer at the Food Shelf. As good works go, it was pretty small potatoes, but it was something, because, as Rob Meehan says, "It takes more than food to fight hunger."

Old Friends, Fresh Interests

Recently, my wife and I hosted a Texas high school friend of mine and his wife. They were up to visit from Washington, D.C. Roger Lewis is a retired professor of architecture who still writes a bi-weekly column on architecture and urban planning for the *Washington Post*. Ellen is a retired lawyer with the Commerce Department, who now teaches school. With them, it's always like playing three-dimensional chess, as conversation with these self-proclaimed news junkies roams around the world and through time and space. There is never a dull moment.

We worked our way through our far-flung children, puzzled over the Middle East maze, reformed health care and smugly agreed that our Priuses were slowing global climate change. Then we turned to our high school yearbooks to marvel at distant and dispersed classmates, and to retell some of our various hijinks, like building a rocket in that Sputnik era.

Like doting parents, my wife and I had fun showing them our city. They had only been here once, in winter's white nakedness. We began with a description by the novelist Henry James 130 years ago. He said, "The vast reach of the Lake and this double mountain view go far to make Burlington a supremely beautiful town."

We took them to a Lake Monsters game in the storied, and possibly doomed, Centennial Field. We told them that the previous owners of this farm club were the Montreal Expos, which had become their home team, the Washington Nationals, where, Roger observed, "the hot dogs cost exactly twice what they do here!"

We sent them up a vibrant Church Street and down to the lakefront with its beehive of activities. I was doubly proud to tell them that the barge on which the boathouse was built had been bought in my own home town in Texas, and towed up through the Hudson River and Champlain Canal to its final mooring.

We sent them to the Lake Champlain Islands. We took them on the Charlotte Ferry, where, coming home from New York under a full moon the light turned the calm waters into shiny blackberry jam.

Finally, we took them to the Intervale, with its river walks, running paths, market gardens, compost project, power plant, and Gardeners Supply. They were impressed enough that I asked Roger, as an urban critic, to write his impressions. Two days later came his email.

He wrote, "Burlington is uniquely blessed to have this green, 'low-lying tract' dedicated entirely to public, agrarian use. I know of no other city encompassing a fertile 'vale' so large—hundreds of acres—and so near downtown, a place where enterprising citizens and organizations can plant gardens, cultivate crops, or keep honeybees, whether for personal or commercial purposes."

He continued, "The morning after I visited the Intervale, I strolled through the Saturday farmers market in Burlington's City Hall Park. I couldn't help wondering which of the fresh products on display—fruits, vegetables, herbs, flowers, cheeses, honey—had come from the Intervale. I left the park thinking about lunch."

Unity and Joy

I've just returned from the fiftieth reunion of my college singing group's tour of Asia. Thirty-eight of the fifty living members attended the gathering in Cambridge, Mass. One even flew in from Australia, and another from Hong Kong. In the summer of 1961, we came, we sang, and musically, we conquered.

Japan, Korea, Taiwan, Hong Kong, the Philippines, Thailand, India, and Greece. We gave thirty-six formal concerts, and numerous informal ones, in sixty days. We performed for crowds of two or three thousand in concert halls and for small groups on street corners or in train stations. We sang in the Taj Mahal, and at the base of the Parthenon. For our repertoire of one hundred pieces we prepared two folk songs for every country, a practice that earned us extra applause at every stop.

One of our singers was totally blind. We all took turns guiding him through the day, explaining what we were seeing. It was a new kind of discipline. We had to describe what an audience looked like, what a pagoda was like, what the North Korean guards looked like at Panmunjom. It intensified an already intense experience.

Like most reunions, this one was built upon the slippery foundations of parallel memories. To anchor our face-to-face exchanges, we had each alumni contribute pictures and recollections to a bound volume that we received upon arrival. Oh, how we pored over its pages, like high school students with new yearbooks. And like a high-school student, I went around and had every attendee sign his name in my book.

But the gathering was much more than twice-told tales. Over two days, we practiced four hours for a concert for family and friends. By e-mail, we had voted for our five favorite songs from the tour. Then one of the tenors, a choral director in his own right, chose thirty songs, which we distilled down to twenty. As we sang our warm-up scales, the scales of age on faces and vocal chords fell away. We were back in Tokyo singing a joint concert with Japanese university students. We were in the Philippine countryside singing in a village school. We were in a Korean palace before seven thousand people.

What we lacked in youthful vocal range we made up for in aging warmth. Most of us had never left music. Two-thirds of us were still singing in serious choruses. One is a composer. Two are professors of music. Unlike many reunions that try (and fail) to recreate the past, we could, in the words of the Christmas carol, "repeat the sounding joy." The concert opened with a sixteenth century motet in honor of our deceased members. Then we did twenty songs, in nine languages, broken into halves so that we could insert more spoken recollections.

We closed with the choir's unofficial theme song, "Glorious Apollo," which contained these words:

"Thus then combining
Hands and hearts joining
Long may continue our unity and joy
Our unity and joy."

Throughout the tour's twenty-five thousand miles, and this reunion, I felt the power of performance—it is better to give than receive.

Thoughts from
Slightly Farther Afield

Ike Fishes Vermont

Not all or even most Presidents have fished as a respite from the lonely cares of the office. But enough did that we can make a few generalizations.

Presidential fishing locations ranged widely, from Georgia sloughs to Pennsylvania streams, from the Texas shore to the Maine Coast, from big rivers in the West to small lakes in the East. They pursued the lordly salmon and the lowly perch, and all species in between. They brought home their limit and they came up empty. They killed fish and released others to fight again. They told the truth, and they lied when they could get away with it. In short, they have been human like the rest of us, for as Herbert Hoover wrote, "All men are equal before fish."

But some of their experiences were distinctly Presidential. Calvin Coolidge had Secret Service agents shoo away anglers from waters reserved for him. Franklin Delano Roosevelt got to fish off a Navy cruiser. And only a former president like Jimmy Carter could compare the theft of two prized fly rods to the loss of a national election.

In June 1955, President Dwight Eisenhower flew into Rutland as part of a "non-political" tour of New England. Sandwiched between an inspection of livestock at the fairgrounds, a luncheon in his honor, and a trip to the Mountain Top Inn in Chittenden for another celebratory meal, the president got in a little fishing on Furnace Brook with famed local fisherman and attorney Milford K. Smith.

Now, Ike was a decent fly fisherman. He'd fished in different parts of the country and even abroad. He eschewed worms for flies and he had a good casting technique. After the trip, Smith rhapsodized in his weekly newspaper column on how well Ike handled the two and one-half ounce bamboo rod. He noted how patiently—and silently—Ike released his fly when an alder branch "seized his fly in an exasperating manner." The pair talked of reels and rods, waters fished and waters wished for, and, as Smith put it, "All those wonderful and useless things that are so much nonsense to the non-fisherman but are meat and drink to the dedicated angler."

Despite all his skill and Smith's attentive guidance, Ike was skunked. It wasn't for lack of effort by his aides. The night before, eager beavers at the U.S. Fish Hatchery in nearby Pittsford stayed up past midnight hauling fat two and three-pound rainbows from the pools to Furnace Brook. Unfortunately, the change in environment was too much of a shock for the fish, and they refused to strike at any of Ike's flies.

Harold Blaisdell, who helped with the stocking, wrote later, "It can be added that local fishermen fared considerably better after the big trout had been at least partially acclimated. Unaware of the nocturnal stocking and prepared for fish only a few inches over the legal limit, these fishermen left the stream in a happy daze, toting trout that wouldn't fit in their creels."

Irish in the Green Mountains

To prepare for this St. Patrick's Day, I've just spanned two millennia of Irish history, in a literary sense. First, I listened again to a tape of Thomas Cahill's rollicking, celebratory history, *How the Irish Saved Civilization,* in which his prose borders on poetry.

Cahill makes the case that when Europe was falling beneath the pillaging assaults of barbarian invaders, a small band of monks retreated to the rocky isle west of Britain, and with pen and vellum made Ireland the safe-house for Western learning until the curtain of darkness began to lift four centuries later. The central figure was, of course, St. Patrick, the Roman slave who became in Cahill's view the first genuine missionary, who ventured beyond the European empire's protection to bring Celtic heathen to Christ.

My second slice of Ireland comes from Vincent Feeney, author, professor, and, forty-plus years ago, immigrant from California. His delightful book, *Finnegans, Slaters, and Stonepeggers: A History of the Irish in Vermont,* doesn't share Cahill's cosmic confidence but it is no less a labor of love. He said, "I knew there was a huge gap in our understanding of Vermont's past, which dealt with *ethnic* history." When he retired, he decided to make this study of the Irish role his contribution. "Someone else will have to do the story of the French, Jews, Welsh, Italians and a few others in Vermont."

He has written a book of facts and folklore, of work and play, and of religion and politics in the Green Mountain State. He describes how the Vermont Irish, as elsewhere, won the badge of citizenship through their Civil War service. He writes of their sports, like collar-and-elbow wrestling, in which contestants tried to throw each other to the ground from a standing position. He relates how as they struggled against Yankee bigotry in many places, they found themselves a social elite in cities like Burlington and Rutland. He tells of how the Irish and French fought for control of the Vermont Catholic Church. He describes the period of 1900–1950 as the golden age of the Irish in Vermont when they created a parallel society of schools, hospitals, and a social hierarchy.

I asked Vince what were two signature contributions of the Irish to

Vermont. First, he said it was the Irish muscle that helped power Vermont's mini-industrial revolution on the railroads and in the slate and marble quarries in the mid-nineteenth century. Second, it was their political championing of the working class in Vermont's cities, which made the cities more liberal than the rural countryside.

My favorite Vermont Irish story is also political. In 1954, Democrat Bob Branon gamely ran for governor, although Vermont had not elected a Democratic governor in almost one hundred years. One evening, while campaigning at a church supper in Fairfield, he seemed to be making progress with a few nods from the audience. But when he asked two women dishing out the apple pie if they could support him, one said, "Oh no, we couldn't do that. We've been Vermonters all our lives."

A Farewell to Wood

A few weeks ago, we put out onto our Burlington curbside the ten logs left over from last year's three-cord wood supply. In two hours those last logs of our last woodpile were gone—presumably to warm some anonymous house or apartment.

It was fitting that this passing of the fireplace torch took place on the spot where thirty years ago, a truck from Hinesburg delivered six cords of wood in eight-foot logs. That fall I spent four months sawing, splitting, and stacking that wood with a Jonsered chain saw, a rented gas-fired splitting maul, and numerous packets of Red Man chewing tobacco.

We began burning wood in the early 1970s when we lived in St. Johnsbury. For one year our only heat was wood. Then oil joined maple and birch on the fire brigade. After that first Burlington year of splitting and spitting, we turned to pre-split logs, but there were always chunks that still needed one more rendezvous with maul or axe. Hauling and stacking firewood became part of the winter's routine. The wood smoke smelled good—forget about its effects on the lungs. The neat stacks made me feel like an architect. For our kids, those woodpiles became fortresses in their backyard wars. Work and political frustrations disappeared in the thwang of maul and wedge. The logs fed the woodstove in a large porch room with no other source of heat. A succession of stoves gave us warmth and turned that room into the center of family activities from meals to games to parties.

I don't know how much money we saved. It depends upon how you value your labor. The benefits were probably more physical and emotional: wood heat as a hobby of the hearth. Then, gradually, in my sixties, my back began to rebel. Of course, heating with wood warms you twice, as the cliché goes. But hauling three cords of wood, log by log, four times, from the driveway to stack, to porch, to fireplace—lost its savor. The logs grew heavier each year, especially after the kids left and we had to do it all ourselves.

This fall, after thirty-six years of trying to balance energy efficiency, environmental responsibility, Vermont self-sufficiency, and convenience, we turned to a gas fireplace. I bid farewell to logs and mauls, splitters and splinters. Farewell to carpet burns and the ubiquitous ash that turned spider webs brown. Farewell to a sore back and smashed toes, to aching arms and banged thumbs. Farewell to Jotul and Hearth-stone, Garrison and Avalon, and the annual visit of a chimney sweep right out of Mary Poppins.

I'll miss the routine, the special warmth of wood, the pocket pride of accomplishment. But for my aging spine my Christmas present came early, and in all this snow, just kept giving.

Wheeler Mountain and Machu Picchu

One of my favorite spots in Vermont is Wheeler Mountain in Barton. It's an easy, if scrambling, hour's hike up its three hundred foot naked granite face. Looking west, you can see Mt. Mansfield and Camel's Hump; to the south, ski trails are finger scratches on Burke's green visage. To the east, a necklace of summer camps ring Lake Willoughby's northern end. Sometimes in the fall geese fly below you as they pass between Wheeler and Mt. Pisgah.

Now fade to black. Four thousand miles to the south of Burke, and eight thousand feet up in the Andes Mountains, one of the great visual clichés of world travel is transformed into a breath-taking marriage of natural beauty and human ingenuity. Above you rises the gigantic green loaf of a mountain you have seen in photos a hundred times before. Beneath your dizzy gaze lies a rectilinear set of sixteenth century stone ruins and terraces that cover a saddle of land, tight as a ski cap. On either side, it's a vertical drop of two thousand feet to the Urubamba River below. All around you, twelve thousand foot high mountains disappear into bands of milk-white clouds.

This is Machu Picchu, the "lost city of the Incas" that Hiram Bingham, the explorer and model for Indiana Jones, discovered eighty-five years ago. Why the Incas built this fabulous village still eludes even the experts. Was it a fortress, a temple city, an academy for royal youth?

We can get closer to how they did it. On a recent trip to Peru, guide books and guides helped me marvel at the construction technique called *ashlar,* in which blocks of stone, often weighing several tons, were fit together so tightly that not even a knife blade could slip between them, nor earthquakes move them. Through the study of their crops, irrigation systems, buildings, and quarried stone, archeologists estimate that only eight hundred people lived here: royalty, priests, and commoners. Those people and perhaps two hundred more were all the mountain could sustain, before the Spaniards destroyed the sixty-year-old Inca empire. They were limited by nature's limits.

As I climbed those hand-carved stone steps and grassy terraces mown by llamas, I realized that modern Peruvians and we Vermonters confront limits of a different sort. What is the aesthetic-carrying capacity of the landscape? Will Wheeler be as wonderful with cell phone towers and windmills and clear-cut forests in the distance? As the hotels creep down the Urubamba River, as roads are cut for bigger buses, and the two thousand visitors a day grows to four or six thousand with their attendant detritus and sewage, what will happen to this world heritage site?

Is there a tipping point when treasure becomes trash? With Oscar Wilde, I wondered, "Does every man kill the thing he loves?" I had no answers, only thanks for the chance to climb Wheeler often and Machu Picchu at least once.

The Battle after the War

Recently, in the basement of St. Andrew's Episcopal Church in Colchester, three dozen people gathered to learn how to help returning National Guard veterans re-adjust to a peaceful society they had left to go to war. The group included clergy, social workers, National Guard personnel, one parent of a deployed soldier, and members of the parish, I among them.

This was the seventh of ten workshops around Vermont led by chaplains from the Veterans Administration (VA) and the Vermont National Guard. Rev. Joseph O'Keeffe of the VA called the re-adjustment process a chair with four legs: physical, mental, social, and spiritual. He said, "Over two hundred years we have trained solders to fight against fearsome foes. We have not learned how to de-program them to live again in a peaceful world. Combat strips away the soldiers' innocence, especially in a war like this, without frontlines and without time off."

The presentation was in vivid contrast to the post-Vietnam experience, when many soldiers came home to open hostility for a hated war. O'Keeffe and Rev. James MacIntyre stressed that civilians should separate their feelings about the war from those for the veterans. When a program called Beyond the Yellow Ribbon urged parishes to become "military-friendly," it meant to regard members of the military as we would any other distressed population in our parish, and to treat the family of a deployed soldier as we would any other family in temporary crisis.

Through slides and discussion of real and hypothetical situations, we learned about the cycle soldiers endure in a combat zone: threat of death or injury to themselves, grief for the death of a comrade, the inner moral conflicts about taking life, and the long-term fatigue of battle.

One slide focused on "8 Battlefield Skills that Make Life in the Civilian World Challenging." In battle, one's focus is on personal safety, trusting a tight group of buddies, making instant decisions, and keeping all your emotions bottled up inside. As one speaker said, "There's not a lot of group therapy in combat."

Speakers gave the audience real situations to ponder. For example, "A twenty-seven-year-old returning veteran won't go to a family picnic without a side-arm." After nervous laughter swept the room, the group got down to analyzing what would make a veteran act this way, and how his family and friends can steer him away from such behavior.

"Don't judge," said O'Keeffe. "Be there and walk with that veteran. Avoid assumptions and just listen very carefully to what they say." Valerie Pallotta, a St. Andrew's parish member whose son Josh is now deployed in Afghanistan, has been volunteering with National Guard support groups the last six months. She calls the other parents she meets, "my battle buddies for life." She is now ready to make our parish veteran-friendly, perhaps with an adopt-a-veteran program.

Despite my grave doubts about the wisdom of these wars, I happily joined Valerie's crusade to make our parish more welcoming toward the returning soldiers whom we sent off to fight.

Opera in the Green Mountains

Unlike my wife, who loves opera, I've only attended a few of the war-horses such as *La Boheme, Madama Butterfly, Carmen,* and *Aida.* Even the advent of translations above the stage moved the needle of my interest only a few degrees. But my indifferent attitude has changed by going to the Middlebury Opera Company. Suddenly, in the richly-refurbished Town Hall Theater, I was there! I was in the orchestra, on the stage, working the lights, singing, and conducting. Or at least it felt that way.

The attractive singers looked their parts. They were mostly young people, on their dream-driven way to bigger stages. Two years ago, when they sang *La Boheme,* they *looked* like love-smitten, starving students. This year, the opera company mounted a rarely-heard work by Georges Bizet. *The Pearl Fishers* required much more willing suspension of disbelief than the torrid love story of Bizet's famous *Carmen.* In a tale of pearl divers in Ceylon, the love triangle is two guys who compete for same priestess. Then one burns down a whole village to save her and his rival from execution.

No matter—the opera contains one of the most famous duets in all of opera. The two young tenors and rivals sang it sitting down, their voices under control. "in the depths of the temple." In that small theater, the pair sounded as powerful as Luciano Pavarotti and Placido Domingo. That theme returned again and again.

As I sat there listening to duets, trios and quartets, I remembered one of my favorite lines from Peter Schaeffer's play, *Amadeus.* The young Mozart was pleading with the Emperor for a commission. "Sire," he said, "In a play, if more than one person speaks at the same time, it's just noise. No one can understand a word. But with music, with music you can have twenty individuals all talking at once, it's not noise, it's a perfect harmony. Only opera can do this!"

Sitting in the second row at Middlebury was better than box seats at the Metropolitan. I was practically on the shoulders of the orchestra members. With four or five familiar faces from the Vermont Symphony Orchestra, it felt a bit like a chamber music concert. I could follow the notes of the violist and trumpeter and almost touch the bow of the double bass. From twenty feet away, I could follow the deft economical gestures of conductor Mark Shapiro as he drew notes, tone, and volume from the musicians. No showy gesture was used. His baton was a magic hat that stirred instrumentalists and singers alike into this delicious bouillabaisse of sound and action.

The performance wasn't perfect—some of the costumes looked thrown together, and the dancing added nothing—but those are nits. This was grand opera because it was grand to be enveloped in an art form on a small stage in Middlebury, Vermont.

What's more, there are only *two* opera companies in Vermont. Next season I'll just have to go check out the Green Mountain Opera Festival in—where else?—the Barre Opera House.

The Stuff to Drink

Almost thirty years ago, I wrote a book about the beginnings of the craft brewing movement. It described what happens when a home brewer gets carried away with the idea of building his own brewery. At the time, there were only six microbreweries in the country. I "sobered up" before I took the final fateful step into the business myself. But hundreds of others pursued their sudsy dreams with such cock-eyed optimism that today there are more than 1,500 small and medium breweries and brewpubs across the land. Nineteen are in Vermont, giving us more breweries per capita than any other state.

This year's Vermont Brewers Festival was dedicated to the memory of Greg Noonan, the owner of the Vermont Pub and Brewery in Burlington, who died last year. In the 1980s he and I worked to pass the law which legalized brew pubs in Vermont. His mantra to all aspiring brewers was simple: "It's all about the beer."

The Vermont brewers, with some help from surrounding states and Quebec, tapped their imaginations and kegs and between them brought 150 different beers to taste. They ranged from the tiny Norwich Inn, Lawson's Finest Liquids in Warren, Rock Art in Morrisville, and Trout River in Lyndonville to the relative behemoths like Long Trail and Magic Hat.

During the brewing revolution, the original styles of beers, stouts, ales, and lagers have morphed into a score of style variations like Belgian ales, German rye beer, fruit beer, smoked beer, and vegetable beer.

Coining weird names is a favorite game for brewers. Among those on tap at this brewers' festival were Camp Ale, APP-GAP Ale, Deadhorse Ale, Noonan's Tribute, Vanilla Espresso Woodchuck Stout, Vermonster, and Boneyard Barley Wine.

The lines at the festival were long enough that you could digest one four-ounce serving, talk about it with others in the line, have a bit of food, and be ready for the next, while remaining under the legal limit. Designated drivers and non-drinkers got in for $5 instead of $25.

There were also education panels where beer, cheese, and chocolate mavens sagely discussed the merits of pairing such foods with drink.

At a few sessions, individual brewers described the genesis of their prize-winning beers.

I ran into lots of people I knew, including a few of my former high school history students. Now that they could drink legally, we could compare notes on the revolution in brewing and share the diversity of beers available in their backyard. In one exchange, I couldn't resist quoting lines from the English poet A.E. Houseman:

"Ale, man, ale's the stuff to drink
For fellows whom it hurts to think."

Burlington Poet Robert Caswell

I first went to Italy when I was six.
It was only a block away.
I set sail from South Champlain Street
And made it all the way to Izzo's Market.

Someone once called Robert Caswell the Poet Laureate of Burlington, and I agree. Any good literature universalizes, or at least broadens, the particular experience or vision of the writer. What is added fun about his poems is that he does this with Burlington people, places, and scenes.

New arrivals in a community have several ways to get a feel for the place—walking, reading back issues of the local newspaper, hanging out in saloons and coffee shops, sniffing around City Hall, enrolling their kids in school. With luck, they find books about the town. In his many collections of poems, Caswell captured the present and the lost past of his natal city. He described "backyards big as all Siberia, now shrunk to a postage stamp." In his requiem to South Champlain Street, done to death by the "urban genocide office," one can visualize what Izzo's Market and Bernadini's Café were like, where "A family wedged in a booth/Was the closest they ever got."

He described sitting out upon the massive iron fire escape at Abernathy's—no longer a store, but just a building. And on Center Street, where the Patra Tea House sits, there worked the shoemaker Hal Sikora, "gaunt as a bone" and "wreathed in Chesterfield smoke."

Caswell's family rented their apartment from the wife of a University of Vermont professor, who was "chauffeured to our door in a late-model Cadillac...She arrived one day/Dressed like visiting nobility/We didn't need/Admired our kitchen/Which we had newly painted/Then went home and raised the rent/By ten dollars." Burlington gave Caswell an Archimedian platform from which to move our minds. But he was ambivalent: "The North End/Is a great place/To come from/But I couldn't live there anymore." In the next lines, he added, "It remains my base/My fundamental/Proving Ground/On whose people/And buildings/I test my assertions/And those of others."

Our society's frenetic mobility has shredded community in so many places. Caswell's poems have re-stitched some of that of Burlington. In his "lover's quarrel" with Burlington, he wrote "Epitaph for a Street (South Champlain Street)," which became as much a prod to the living as a celebration of the dead. Of urban renewal, he wrote,

Such madness in the bulldozer community.
They could have re-built with imagination.
The new cathedrals could have faced
The new courthouse, a reminder each to each.

Robert Caswell reminded us all that the vitality of Burlington, or of any city, depends upon flesh and blood as much as financial and commercial security.

The Life of O.O. Howard

In the Pine Grove section of Burlington's Lakeview Cemetery is a simple headstone less than a foot high. The inscription reads, "O.O. HOWARD," and underneath are two simple stars. This is the grave of Major General Oliver Otis Howard, who died in Burlington just over one hundred years ago. During a forty-four-year career in the Army and beyond, he waged war and peace and racial reconciliation. A biography of him is appropriately entitled, *The Sword and the Olive Branch*.

Howard was born in Maine in 1830. As a devout Christian, he debated whether to go to a seminary or to West Point. Even after graduating fourth in his West Point class, he thought of becoming a minister. The attack on Fort Sumter ended the debate. He fought through the entire Civil War, from Bull Run to Sherman's march to the sea. He lost an arm at the battle of Seven Oaks. His religious beliefs as a commander were so open and persistent that with compliment and snicker alike, he was dubbed the "Christian General."

At war's end, based upon his reputation as both hero and humanitarian he was named the first Commissioner of the Freemans's Bureau, a de facto social service agency established to help freed slaves obtain education, health care, and jobs. In this key department of reconstruction, Howard battled Southern intransigence and terror, accusations of politicking in the Bureau, picayune budgets, and President Andrew Johnson's opposition.

When he took the job, he wrote, "The rights of the freedman, which are not yet secured to him, are the direct reverse of the wrongs committed against him. I never could detect the shadow of a reason why the color of the skin should impair the right to life, liberty, and the pursuit of happiness."

In the midst of these heavy duties, Howard and a group of others established an all-black college in Washington D.C. that became, in his honor, Howard University. He served as its first president from 1868 to 1874. Still in uniform, he was sent to the West to fight in the Indian wars. He was able to negotiate a peace settlement with the Apache chief Cochise, but he took up the sword to chase Chief Joseph of the Nez

Perce tribe in 1879.

After serving as superintendent of West Point and commander of various military districts in the East, Howard retired to Burlington in 1894. In part this was because one son, an Army regular, had been sent to restore nearby Fort Ethan Allen as a military post. For his last fifteen years, Howard was an indefatigable lecturer and fundraiser for various causes and colleges. He wrote eight books, four for adults and four for children.

It was the establishment of schools under the Freeman's Bureau that Howard considered one of his greatest accomplishments. Of this, he wrote, "The burden of my efforts...may be condensed into the words: educate the children. That was the relief needed. Is it not always the relief which in time becomes a permanency?"

Ideas and Ideals
from Here and There

Inventing Our Family Truth

In the last few months my older brother and I have been assembling our family history. We've both sailed past the age of seventy with only minor cuts and abrasions. But our father died on his seventy-third birthday, and our other brother died at eighteen. So the candle of mortality cast its guttering light on this project.

In family history, as in all writing, we discovered there are only three questions: Who's your audience? What to put in? What to take out?

Since we didn't plan to publish our history, we only needed to please ourselves, as well as our children, grandchildren, cousins, their cousins—well, you get the idea.

So what did we include? The writer Russell Baker said the autobiographer/family historian knows too much: the whole iceberg, not just the tip. First we reviewed what we knew, such as the stories passed down for years at the family dinner table, then what we had, like family letters, and finally how much research we wanted to do. All the while, we kept in mind that information inevitably varies with generations. Some are replete with records, and others are as uninformative as gravestones.

We had waited too long to interview our parents or grandparents (a wonderful resource if you still have them) so we turned to our cousins, who see family events from a different vantage point. Some stories didn't need much context; other ones demanded it. We gathered a wealth of anecdotes, travel stories, and family memories. Then we selected the bits that interested us most, and could perhaps show something of why we are who we are.

We've been lucky in the written record. Our father's brother wrote a thirty-page history of their family's emigrant story. My mother made a similar record of her early life and ancestors. Then, finally, it was time to tell the stories of our own lives. Here withered grass turned into lush weeds and vivid flowers, and we were drowning in material. Choosing what to include was much tougher.

So we tried to decide what we would tell a best friend if we were trading stories. And we took a longer view, shifting our audience from children to grandchildren and beyond, trying not to get bogged down in too much detail, and being as concrete as possible. We added the honey and vinegar of a few successes and a few failures. And we tried to find the right tone between a tinny false modesty and brassy bragging.

It was fun to do, this treasure hunt of part memory, part research. And we got to decide how much to smudge our own page of history. Some family stories are mostly myth anyway, an accounting of things that never really were but will always be.

The result never purported to be a memoir, which requires much more labor and genuine creation. Indeed, the title of William Zinsser's revealing collection of essays about the memoir as a literary form is *Inventing The Truth*.

Adventures in Sarajevo

For fifteen years I used events in Sarajevo to illustrate two blood-drenched bookends of the twentieth century. The assassination there of the Austrian Arch-Duke Franz Ferdinand on June 28, 1914 was arguably the most important event in the twentieth century; to visit that very site was like going to Gettysburg or Cedar Creek for the Civil War buff.

I shivered as I stood on the Latin Bridge over the Mijacka River and read again how five young co-conspirators, one by one, failed to reach their target. Then, incredibly, the driver of the Arch-Duke's open car took a wrong turn and stopped right in front of nineteen-year old Gavrilo Princip, a Bosnian Serb. Princip stepped to the running board and put bullets into the Arch Duke and his wife Sophia.

In only five weeks, the Great Power alliance dominoes toppled, and Europe exploded into a general war that eventually took fourteen million lives and re-arranged the maps of Europe and the Middle East. Then, from this same spot on a river no wider than the Winooski in Montpelier, my eyes rose first to a few pockmarked buildings and then to two mountain ranges of three thousand feet which seemed to arch over the city.

In the early 1990s Serb gunners commanded those heights during a three-year long siege that killed more than ten thousand people, including a thousand children. They shelled the city with indiscriminate artillery, rocket, and mortar fire. More murderously, like the camp commander in Schindler's list, they used humans for target practice. "Shoot slowly, continuously, drive them mad!" were orders from the Serb commander Ratko Mladic, who is still allegedly hiding in Serbia.

In this most cosmopolitan city in the Balkans, which had hosted the winter Olympics in 1984, every act of peaceful human exchange was snuffed out. Opening a window, crossing a street, or standing in a market line put people's lives in jeopardy. While the men fought, mothers had to decide if they would risk death to get water for their families. The siege was only broken by NATO air strikes and a UN resolution to force the Serbs to pull back.

But my grim day of history ended on a lighter note. On my way to catch a bus back to Croatia, I had fifteen minutes to take pictures along a tramline, dubbed Sniper's Alley, because it was a favorite hunting ground for Serb gunners to fire at civilians dodging between wrecked streetcars to cross the open land.

Suddenly a cop appeared at my side and motioned that I follow him to a temporary police station in front of a large building under construction. This did not look good. Several other cops surrounded me. "Your passport please," said one with good English. "You shouldn't be taking picture here."

"Why?" I asked.

"It's an embassy."

"Whose?"

"Yours!"

Thank goodness for a digital camera. When I showed them that all the pictures were indeed of the tram line, they waved me on good-naturedly. I made the bus with five minutes to spare.

Self-Deliverance

A number of years ago, I helped precipitate the mud fight over who was a Real Vermonter and who was a Flatlander. The battle went on until Bob Sherman, a journalist-turned-lobbyist, ended the debate with the common-sensical suggestion that a Real Vermonter was someone who planned to die here.

This year, the legislature is debating an equally common-sensical bill called Death with Dignity, which will help Vermonters say how and when they will die. The Death with Dignity bill proposes to allow, subject to appropriate safeguards, a mentally competent person diagnosed as having less than six months to live to request a prescription, which if taken, would hasten the dying process. The crucial part is that patients are in control over the timing and manner of dying, if they wish to exercise this choice.

The bill is packed with safeguards to allow people that choice and end in the most grateful, dignified, and informed way possible. This is free will at its most fundamental. Twenty years ago, my terminally ill eighty-three-year-old mother took her own life. In this act she had the approval of her family and her doctor. For twenty years before that, she had told her family, "When I cease to appreciate the gift of life, I'm leaving on my terms, not yours, or the doctors, or, God forbid, the lawyers."

She wasn't a hypochondriac, morbid, or deranged. She was simply determined that her life would not be prolonged in pain and suffering in a medical or legal stranglehold. My mother was one tough woman. Because she lived life to the fullest, she said she was always ready to check out, when that time came. And she was. She was also fortunate to have a sympathetic doctor who knew her well enough to share in her thoughtful and prayerful judgment of when that moment came.

Her doctor gave her a prescription of sleeping pills, and she stored them up. When their due date was up, she renewed them, the same way she had the fire extinguishers re-charged. For twenty years, she kept "my pills" on the second shelf of the drug cabinet.

The Death with Dignity bill before the Vermont Legislature legalizes and encourages this kind of open, intelligent, legal conversation about end-of-life choices between doctor and a terminally ill, mentally competent patient like my mother. She had to do on the sly what should be the legal right of all qualifying Vermonters. Let's take this conversation out of the guilt-shrouded darkness and into the open where it can be supervised, regulated, and available to all who qualify. Let's have a bill which protects merciful doctors who follow the prescribed protocols and safeguards shown to function flawlessly in the State of Oregon.

My mother liked to say she didn't have much of a sense of humor, but in her self-deliverance she delivered one memorable line. When I asked her how she was going to do the deed, she said she would put the pills into a bowl of ice cream, "Häagen-Dazs," she said, "Not, I'm afraid, Ben and Jerry's."

A Life-Changing Bet

The first time I heard this story was during the Thanksgiving holidays, while deer hunting with my father and two brothers in West Texas.

My father's father, Josef Maresh, was born in Zemberk, Bohemia, in what is now the Czech Republic. We share a birthday—November 8 —me in 1940, he in 1856. After four years in Berlin training to be a shoemaker, he returned to Zemberk to find a draft notice from the Austro-Hungarian army. Unwilling to serve the emperor, he fled to the United States. He arrived in eastern Montana in 1877, a year after Custer's Last Stand, and found work as a cowboy rounding up horses to sell to the British Army for its wars in Southern Africa. After two years on the plains, he got a chance to use his leather-working skills making shoes and mule harnesses in the mining town of Marysville, about twenty miles from the territorial capital of Helena.

He worked very hard for ten years and put half his savings into a bank in Helena, and half into grubstaking miners. Now, grubstaking was that peculiar combination of a lottery and welfare system of lending money to miners in return for a share of their discoveries, which for most miners were exceedingly rare.

One night, however, there came a rap on his window, and one of the miners he'd invested in told him breathlessly, "They struck the mother lode at the Drumlummon mine. Get out of bed and get to Helena and buy some of their stock before the word gets out."

My grandfather saddled up and rode into Helena. At 9 a.m. he surprised a clerk at the bank by pulling out all his savings, about five hundred dollars. At 9:30 he was at the mine office to buy what stock he could. At noon, news of the strike reached Helena and the stock doubled in price that day and tripled again by the end of the year. When he sold his stock the next year, he was able to go back to Zemberk, marry, and bring his wife to Montana where he and his brother founded a meat company and small amusement park on Helena's outskirts. These ventures prospered enough for him to send the three children to college: in my father's case to Massachusetts Institute of Technology.

My father, who never gambled except at gin rummy with his sons, always spoke in grateful awe of the life-changing bet his father had made.

Macedonia with the
Vermont National Guard

I just spent a week in Macedonia with the Vermont National Guard, as a civilian. I knew a little about the country. Until 1994, Macedonia was one of the republics of the former Yugoslavia. I knew that Mother Teresa, an Albanian Catholic, was born in the capital of Skopje. And I knew that Macedonia and Greece are arguing over the name of Macedonia, and the fame of Alexander the Great. Little else.

Macedonia is about Vermont's size, but with four times our population. It's craggy and mountainous like Vermont, and looks even more rural because so many people live in the cities, six hundred thousand in the capital of Skopje. The State Partnership Program was the brainchild of Colin Powell, former chair of the Joint Chiefs of Staff, and later Secretary of State. He aimed to link state national guards with the former subject nations of the Soviet Union (and later the disintegrating Yugoslavia) and bring them into NATO, the North Atlantic Treaty Organization. Over fifteen years, the Partnership project has grown to involve almost all states and sixty-one countries. During that time, Vermont and Macedonia have carried out over six hundred different exchanges with several thousand participants in both countries.

These exchanges are on three levels: military-to-military, military-to-civilian, and civilian-to- civilian. On the military-to-military level, two examples were to train Macedonian Army military police platoons to take part in international peacekeeping missions and to help build up a non-commissioned officer corps within the army, which didn't exist under the Yugoslav system.

On this trip, which was one of the largest military-to-civilian exchanges to date, Vermont Guard engineers helped do environmental assessments of school renovation projects. In other projects, three doctors helped establish a tele-medical link between Skopje hospitals and Fletcher Allen. Lawyers from the U.S. Attorney's office and Department of Homeland Security lectured on how to combat money-laundering. Officials from the state Parks and Historic Sites departments worked with their counterparts on tourist initiatives. My cluster in agricultural businesses focused on helping the Macedonians improve their wine and specialty crop exports, including honey, my expertise.

"This is not training, or foreign aid in the traditional sense," said Major John Geno of the Vermont National Guard. "This is about building relationships with people in shared activities and classes on topics where Macedonians and Vermonters can learn from each other." Personally, I had fun hanging out with Macedonia beekeepers and meeting people from a new country. But it was also fun to work with these Guardsmen and other civilians in a foreign policy blend of what Harvard professor Joseph Nye calls "*hard* power" and "*soft* power."

You never really know how you are perceived when you go abroad, but I agree with assistant U.S. Attorney Bill Darrow, who says, "I hope the Macedonians learned that we care, that we are not as arrogant as we may appear, that we try to keep open minds, and that we are eager to discuss common interests and learn about their country."

Curtains

Last week, town volunteers gathered in the Canaan Historical Society to help a team of conservators re-hang an eighty-year-old 10 x 15 painted theater. The curtain's still-vibrant colors depict a silhouetted jazz band playing against a backdrop of party balloons advertising Leon's Café, Beecher Falls Garage, Cummins Chevrolet, and a gaggle of other local businesses in the northeastern corner of Vermont.

For the last ten years my wife had directed a project to repair scores of historic theater curtains like this one, painted between 1880 and 1940 and hung in Vermont's town halls, community theaters, opera halls, and Grange halls from Canaan to Pawlet and from Richford to Guilford. These curtains were used as backdrops for plays and vaudeville in the days before television and radio.

The team of conservators has now finished over 130 of the 177 known curtains across the state. These large curtains, averaging 12 x 20 feet in dimension, have been rescued from lofts, attics, closets, and even trash barrels. The team carefully avoids the term "restore." Instead, they speak of stabilizing the curtains, cleaning them with dry sponges and vacuum cleaners, mending tears and judiciously in-painting water-stains or the mended tears. In every town, conservators specializing in textiles, paper, and painting find local volunteers who enthusiastically join the work on "their" curtains.

On these broad expanses of muslin are displayed marvelous imaginary scenes of European lakes and castles, American coastlines and Western caravans, and even a chariot race in the Roman Colosseum. Some show identifiable Vermont locations like Lake Willoughby and Mt. Ascutney, and others depict imagined modern streets devoid of people and vehicles, as if the painters were practicing perspective. Some curtains like that in Canaan were primarily advertising media. For today's viewer, it's fun to scan them for the names of druggists, feed stores, banks, fuel, or car dealers still in business.

The painters were both locals and itinerants who came through town to paint curtains and then move on. The most prolific and fascinating artist was Guilford-born Charles Henry who did over forty paintings and died in North Ferrisburgh in 1918. He would arrive in a town, paint one or more curtains to be used as sets for a play he would write, and perform with members of his own family.

Wounded by time and neglect, but repaired with care, these curtains are back on display for school plays, musicals, dances, variety shows, town meetings and even weddings. A few, too fragile for hanging, have been put into deep storage. But most are helping to rejuvenate some of the town centers across the states. As Rick Kerschner, a conservator at the Shelburne Museum said, "People talk a lot of Vermont's sense of community. Well, the performances and gatherings in front of these curtains helped build that community, long before radio, television and cheap gas put people in their own little envelopes."

Maybe the high price of gas will also help bring more people back downtown, where the suspended worlds of the past will spur today's imagination.

The Marriage of Muscle and Mind

At noon today, some sixteen thousand runners will head east from the Hopkinton, Massachusetts green for the 112th running of the Boston Marathon. A twinge of melancholy will flutter in my stomach, because I won't be there for this most famous of distance races and the longest continuous sporting event in the world.

Four times I ran Boston, along with twenty-five other marathons. This is the Boston of Heartbreak Hill, the famous Johnny Kelly, and the infamous Rosie Ruiz. For Vermont runners, it's a magical rite of spring, sometimes the first chance we have to wear shorts. I'll miss its crowd of two million, the Dixieland band in Framingham, the cathedrals of cheers at Wellesley and Boston College, and finally dragging myself over the line on Boylston Street in what the Czech runner Emil Zatopek called the "most pleasant exhaustion I have ever known."

For fifteen years, spring and fall marathons structured my exercise year in increments of three months and five hundred to six hundred miles of distance run. Central to that training were two Saturday morning three-hour runs with a trio of buddies. Ralph Swenson, an administrator at UVM, Rick Peyser, director of social advocacy at Green Mountain Coffee Roasters, and Phil Coleman, a chemistry teacher at my school.

We were roughly the same age (although I was both the oldest and the slowest), roughly the same educational level, and roughly the same politics. Over twelve years in sun, rain, snow, and sleet, with temperatures between -10 and 80+, we roamed the bike paths, roads, and trails of Burlington, South Burlington, Shelburne, and Williston. Talking non-stop, we treated these jaunts as seminars on the move, panting proof that a sound mind still springs from a sound body.

Oh, we would touch on past races or injuries or the ache of the day. But the bulk of the conversation was heavy and high-minded stuff from school to politics, art, music, literature, families, and even sports. Humor was both a diversion and a prod to keep each other going. The worst sin was not pride but self-pity.

Ralph was our running guru because outside our presence he

was obsessive. In thirty years, he put more than one hundred thousand miles on his long legs, and ran over a hundred races of marathon distance and longer. As Rick puts it, he's "the physically fit sage who combines an encyclopedic knowledge of running, runners, races, and injuries with a holistic analytical perspective on running and the world."

I'll miss the focus that marathons provided, but I'll still join this rumpled, ragged gang on Saturday mornings for runs of lesser distance, at slower times: a weekly marriage of muscle and mind.

Graduation Speech

When you think about success, you have to think about failure first.

The most obvious kind of failure is to flunk an exam. You didn't study, the questions were too hard, or maybe you just had a bad day. Then there are athletic losses. Most of my varsity teams at high school had losing seasons. We grew tired of the explanation that somehow we were "building character." But that was our lot.

A third type of failure is based on the belief that once you've chosen a course, job, profession, or even just an opinion, you should stick with it come hell or high water. The *New York Times* recently ran a piece about a lawyer who threw over a six-figure income to repair motorcycles because he wanted concrete fulfillment with his hands and mind.

Failure can also be caused by forces beyond our individual control. The economy today is shedding jobs by the millions, and the people affected did everything conventional wisdom, morality, and economics told them to do. But they're still pounding the pavement looking for jobs.

We can also fail to measure up to, or achieve, our own aspirations. By that definition, I myself am a three-time failure. In the eight years after I left high school, I tried to become a Foreign Service Officer, then a banker, then a lawyer. In the first case, the State Department rejected me. In the second case, I rejected banking, and the third case was a draw—I hated law school and law school didn't like me much either.

I can joke about it now, but at the time, I was pretty devastated. Then I fell into writing and journalism, followed by politics and teaching, through blind, dumb luck, not due to any planning on my part. I'm not talking about deliberate or reckless failure, but the kind that comes in spite of your hardest labors and most fervent desires.

Of the four definitions of failure in the Oxford University Dictionary, my favorite says, "to become exhausted, to give way under trial, to fall short in performance or attainment." I like it because it assumes you've tried—hard—and I think that's the key to success.

There's a YouTube clip of an ad in which Michael Jordan arrives for a game. As he walks slowly toward the players' entrance, out of the darkness you hear him say: "I have missed more than nine thousand shots in my career...I've lost almost three hundred games...twenty-six times I've been trusted to take the winning shot and missed. I have failed over and over and over again in my life, and that's why I succeed."

In his book *Life on the Mississippi,* Mark Twain described a boat pilot who applied for a job. He said he deserved the post because he knew where all the sandbars were. The captain asked, "How?"

"I hit 'em," the man replied, and got the job.

Remembering Studs Terkel

I heard his voice three years before I saw his face. It was a raspy, gravelly growl that sounded like the cranky engine of a tramp steamer. And it belonged to Studs Terkel, the chronicler of ordinary Americans in ordinary and extraordinary times, who died last week at the age of ninety-six.

When I first moved to Chicago in the '60s for graduate school, I listened to his morning talk show almost daily. Later, as a reporter for the *Chicago Sun-Times*, I met him at the Billy Goat Tavern near the paper where he and the legendary columnist Mike Royko held court. He always dressed the same way: red and white checked shirt, red tie, a blazer, charcoal trousers, and a big cigar that he waved around for emphasis, a veritable baton of speech.

By that time he was famous for his first oral history, "Division Street America." Through four decades, more than twenty books poured from his tapes and typewriter, with bestsellers such as *Hard Times, Working,* and *The Good War,* each built upon scores of interviews with average people. He was to words what his friends Pete Seeger and Woody Guthrie were to music, a troubadour of the little guy.

Last Sunday I shared an impromptu wake for Studs with Judy Kelly of Burlington, who knew Studs and his wife Ida for over fifty years. Studs had worked for Judy's father in 1940s radio shows like "Jack Armstrong" and "Ma Perkins." Judy said, "You have to remember that Studs began his professional career as an actor. He would get into a role and treat others as fellow actors, as equals. His interviews were really dialogues."

She reminded me that Studs always asked big open-ended questions, and let his subjects go as far as they could. Then he would jump in with his own thoughts. He'd also modulate his voice to fit the person and the subject. Among the guests on his Chicago show were luminaries like John Kenneth Galbraith, Aaron Copeland, Oliver Sacks, and Bob Dylan, as well as many less august figures, myself among them.

I appeared on his program to discuss a book I was writing about coal miners in West Virginia. At first, I was tongue-tied just to be in the

60

same studio with Studs Terkel, but he was used to that. He had a way of embracing you with his voice, his questions and his knowledge of the topic. In my case, when he began talking about people like Mother Jones and Big Bill Haywood and Eugene Debs, I relaxed.

Ten years later, when an economist friend and I wrote a book about workplace democracy, we titled it *Working Together,* in his honor. Studs once told an interviewer, "The thing I'm able to do, I guess, is break down walls. If they think you're listening, they'll talk. It's more of a conversation than an interview." His limitless curiosity and patience allowed him to extract gems of human experience from commonplace ores.

Fittingly, his chosen epitaph was "Curiosity did not kill *this* cat."

Coffee and Honey in Oaxaca

I'm on the board of Coffee Kids, a charity which gives scholarships to Latin youths, and promotes economic diversification for coffee-growing families in Latin America in order to lessen their dependence upon this widely and wildly traded commodity.

Four weeks ago, several board members got to tag along and watch how one of our partner organizations, the Center to Support the Popular Movement in Oaxaca (CAMPO), works with indigenous farmers in a remote region of the Mexican state of Oaxaca. The twenty-year-old group began as a social and quasi-political organization to help indigenous people battle social and economic oppression at the local and national levels. Ten years ago, they switched their focus to technical assistance, environmental protection, and women's empowerment in sixty rural communities spread across the entire state.

In a poor land, these are some of poorest. Illiteracy is over 40 percent. The average wage is less than four dollars per day. In Santo Tomas Texas, a community of a hundred families, we saw a microcosm of the challenges that CAMPO and the people face. First of all, it's remote, six hours from the capital of Oaxaca on white-knuckle mountain roads with enough hairpin turns to run a beauty shop. Political scientists and sociologists would quail at the overlapping government, ambiguous land tenure rights, and complex social customs.

Undaunted, the CAMPO staff has helped develop a range of activities to supplement the coffee income. There were greenhouses to extend the growing season. Some farmers were producing rare and valuable honey from stingless bees. They practice worm farming to produce organic compost. There was chicken raising and small-scale fish farming.

To me, the most fascinating experience was to observe the communal discussions between CAMPO staff and the villagers. The CAMPO staff knew they must walk a fine line between inviting questions and giving advice, between nurturing leaders and anointing them. As we all do, they struggled to find the right words to use in constructive criticism. Just as importantly, they had to know when to be silent and listen.

Gradually, people spoke up. First, it was objective matters, like repairing greenhouses, or building a community center. Then they moved on to some of their fears. The coffee crop was way down this year, said one man. "Some people have migrated to the city. A couple of farmers came close to suicide." They knew they needed alternatives but as one said, "We are slaves to coffee. It's what we know. We want to improve the quality of our coffee to get a better price."

One supplement to coffee income was honey production, both from European bees and from the local stingless bees. A group of women who had been rebuffed by the males had formed their own group of beekeepers. One woman said, "The bees sting me. So what! I can earn good money from selling the honey!"

One young man, about twenty-five, was just back from the States where he worked for six years. After thanking CAMPO, he said, "I came back to live and help in this village. The U.S. is a beautiful place, but you suffer a lot there. I'm glad to be home."

Opinions and Observations

Becoming an Intellectual

As this most recent political campaign nears the end, with its flood of claims and counter-claims, and the undecided are left to sort it all out, I'm reminded of one of the joys of teaching high school history. It was watching kids learn to do their *own* kind of sorting out as their minds matured. I didn't have a lot to do with it. That's the way we all develop—to go from concrete to abstract thinking in those mid-teen years. Nevertheless, I enjoyed telling them that my small contribution to their learning would be to turn them all into "intellectuals."

When they looked at me suspiciously, I said all it means is that you will be at home with ideas. The key to being an intellectual, I said, is learning how to think critically. I was raised to believe ideas are important, that what you do with your mind was at least as important as what you do physically. I was also taught maturity does not bring certitude, but the ability to live with ambiguity and complexity. While many questions might be clear, most answers are murky. Not for nothing does my license plate read THINK.

Thinking *is* hard work, I promised the students. It means being curious about and tolerant of others' ideas. It requires patience to follow or develop arguments. It means acknowledging, probably privately, that we can be wrong. In a nation with a streak of anti-intellectualism going back to frontier populism and religious fundamentalism, it's well to remember that ideas are not tablets of stone, carved once and forever, by some divine hand. Our history of preaching and building democracy gave us each a mental hammer and chisel to improve our political system—or destroy it.

I enjoyed teaching reflective thinking. Not only was I able to watch mental flowers bloom, I also had to do a little fertilizing. Students came to us high school teachers believing in the steadfast absolutes of good and bad, fair and unfair. We tried to show them the shades of gray. In debates, we pushed them to see the other side. We taught about the tricks of dishonest argument, such as attacks on the person, not the idea, guilt by association, stereotyping and sloganeering. I was so conscious of the power of suggestion in a teacher's opinion that I bit my tongue until it scarred over.

In European history, we set up mock trials, one to try Columbus for crimes against humanity and the other a reenactment of the Versailles Treaty charging Germany with responsibility for World War I. In Art Appreciation, we followed a four-stage process that first described what an object looked like, what it was made of and what the artist might have had in mind. Only then did they get to say if they liked it or not, and tell why.

Finally, we tried to discuss a quotation each day. My favorite aphorism of wisdom and ambiguity was from the theologian Reinhold Niebuhr: "Man's capacity for justice makes democracy possible, but man's capacity for injustice makes democracy necessary." It's a quote worth re-visiting in the twilight of the current political season.

A Commons Without Tragedy

Forty years ago in a seminal essay entitled, "The Tragedy of the Commons," the biologist Garrett Hardin gave the nascent environmental movement its abiding parable and conundrum. How does society divide limited resources?

The image of the commons comes from the medieval practice of a common grazing land open to all. Economically speaking, it is in the immediate self-interest of each herder to add more of his cows to that common land. Gradually, however, the commons loses its capacity to sustain the ever higher demand on its grass. Eventually the entire resource is depleted, even though such destruction was in no one's long-term interest.

Ever since Hardin wrote the essay, ecologists and political scientists have applied the theory to grazing, forests, fisheries, wildlife protection, water resources, irrigation systems, and outdoor recreation. The term "reverse commons" came into use to conceptualize private pollution of public waterways, the sea, and the atmosphere.

Hardin's thesis was controversial from the start. Advocates of population control and limits to economic growth hailed the essay. Conservatives used his theory to argue for greater private property rights. Today, people talk of the "new" commons in relation to global climate change, the internet, even intellectual property.

As an ordinary citizen I have found Hardin's thesis a fruitful touchstone for looking at the clash over resources between individual self-interest and that of the collective, locality, state, nation and globe. At what point does use became over-use? Some guidelines for answering this question appeared in a recent article in the *Economist* magazine. "What you take out must equal what you put in. Everyone has to have a say in rule-making. Use has to be compatible with the underlying health of commons." In other words, "First, do no harm."

To mull these issues further, I went to see Robert Manning, a professor in the Rubenstein School of Environment and Natural Resources at UVM. He has spent much of his career testing Hardin's theory in practice. His specialty is the national park system. "I'm so happy he used the national parks as an example of protecting the commons," he said. "We can love the parks to death." But Manning thinks Hardin was too pessimistic about the power of human nature to override any common interests. He sees enlightened self-interest, even altruism, having a significant influence in this process.

Manning's life's work has been to crystallize that idea of limits in the management and stewardship of the parks. The key device has been a permit system built upon the principle Hardin enunciated, which is "mutual coercion mutually agreed upon." Indeed, in 2007, Manning wrote a book called *Parks and Carrying Capacity: Commons without Tragedy.*

War Forever

Not long ago, Secretary of Defense Robert Gates gave a speech that decried the growing disconnect between the general population and the volunteer soldiers, who have been fighting the longest large-scale military operations in our history. He said that for most Americans, the wars remain an abstraction.

His solution was to ask that more universities bring back ROTC to train more officers. I agree with him, and believe that this remoteness of the military is both a cause and effect in the ever-growing militarization of our foreign policy. It has led to a state where, as the saying goes, "If the only tool you have is a hammer, you tend to see every problem as a nail."

In the last year we have seen a surge in Afghanistan, and a deepening military involvement inside Pakistan. We're sending naval ships into the Yellow Sea to rattle the North Korean cage. We're squeezing the Chinese in the South China Sea. Yemen threatens to be another battleground. And all this comes against a background drum roll to bomb Iran.

In the worst economic crisis since the Great Depression, the military budget was sacrosanct. Both political parties were complicit in this, for they often saw defense spending as a big boost to local economies. And some of the loudest voices in a fragmented media equate patriotism with a kind of chauvinistic militancy. We now have more than seven hundred military bases ringing the globe. Do they really make us any safer? But which president or Congress would dare dismantle them? Psychologically speaking, whereas in past wars Americans learned to fear specific enemies, today we have conditioned ourselves to live in a general, ill-defined state of fear.

The global War on Terror promises to have us at war forever. General David Petraeus himself has said that Afghanistan, "is the kind of fight we're in for the rest of our lives and probably our kids' lives." Furthermore, today's wars are cheap. They require us to spend only 2 percent of our gross national product, compared to 36 percent during World War II. "The army is at war, but the country is not," says David

M. Kennedy, the Stanford University historian.

What to do? Well, I say, follow Gates' logic to the end and reinstate the draft. Make all subject to military (or civilian) service. Wars on this scale are not games for presidents and Congress to play while the rest of us party on with "American Idol" and the National Football League, or have hissy fits over airport pat-downs.

Andrew Bacevich is a Boston University professor and Vietnam veteran who lost a son to a roadside bomb in Iraq. "The draft," he wrote recently, "offers a more equitable distribution of sacrifice in war time. No longer will rural Americans, people of color, recent immigrants, and members of the working class fill the ranks of the armed forces in disproportionate numbers. With conscription, the children of the political elite and of the well-to-do will once again bear their fair share of the load."

On Torture and Terror

As Vermont's Senator Patrick Leahy leads the charge to investigate the use of torture, also known as "harsh interrogation tactics," in the fight against terrorism, a former Vermonter has just released a film about kidnapping, torture, and murder in Argentina in the late 1970s and early 1980s.

Peter Sanders, a UVM graduate in 1992, and the son of an Argentine musicologist mother and an Academy Award-winning filmmaker father, grew up in Argentina and Texas. His film, "The Disappeared," documents one heartrending practice during the so-called dirty war between 1976 and 1983, when Argentina was ruled by a military junta. After a left-wing terrorist campaign of assassination of government officials and military leaders, a group of generals and admirals overthrew the civilian government. In retaliation, perhaps as many as thirty thousand labor leaders, political activists and university students were kidnapped, tortured, and murdered. Many simply disappeared into unmarked graves, or more gruesomely, were drugged and thrown out of military planes into the South Atlantic. While living in Buenos Aires, Sanders became interested in what happened to the babies born to some of these disappeared students. He focused on Horacio Pietragalla, a young man in his twenties who was raised by the maid of a police official. Like an unfolding detective story, Sanders documents how Horacio became suspicious about his true parentage, and eventually through DNA evidence learned that his birth parents had been arrested and murdered after he was born, and that the police official who took him had probably been one of the torturers.

With a deft camera and smooth one-on-one style, Sanders weaves together documentary footage of the protests, the torture chambers, interviews with the maid, Horacio's surviving foster family members, journalists, the group of mothers who launched a public protest about their lost children, and even some unrepentant military and police officers.

When I was in Argentina in April, I talked to a woman who had been a university student in Buenos Aires during this period. As soon as I asked her about the dirty war, the words poured out of her.

"We didn't know, but we should have; but then we were so isolated in those days. We went to Catholic schools, not to the public university. We worked in the slums doing good work, we thought. We thought that was enough. Politics was for someone else. We believed the government papers when they said the biggest threats were from the urban guerillas. We only saw the dead bodies of government officials killed. It wasn't until friends came from Europe, and said the newspapers there were full of stories about the disappeared, that we began to doubt."

I told her about Senator Leahy's truth commission proposal and the opposition to it from left and right. "Maybe you should put some of the officials on trial!" she said.

"Boy, I think Leahy would be delighted just to get the Truth Commission approved."

She thought for a moment. "Well, it's important for a country to go through this soul-searching after events like this. You'll have to decide best how to proceed."

Conspiracy and Facts

Conspiracy theories like the birther movement are a hardy perennial in America's historical garden. They arise in both bad and good, although fear and uncertainty are strong fertilizers. Sometimes they can be entertaining, like the novels of Dan Brown. Others can be lethal.

Such practices got an early start in our history. By some measures, the Salem witch trials in late seventeenth century Massachusetts might be considered a conspiracy in which a toxic mixture of politics, religion, and personal grudges spread suspicion and judicial murder across the colony. In the 1920s, none other than Henry Ford distributed five hundred thousand copies of an infamous forged anti-Semitic tract, which alleged that a Jewish conspiracy was trying to take over the world.

When I was growing up, UFOs were said to be circling above, martians were thought to be landing below, and the government allegedly wasn't doing anything about it. Still other people claimed that putting fluoride in the drinking water was a plot to weaken us for a Communist take-over. Then came the Kennedy assassination, which, in the words of one researcher, "democratized" conspiracy theories and created an industry of what you might call assassinology.

Conspiracy theories in this country often have merged with anti-intellectualism. It's not just suspicion of "pointy-headed intellectuals" on college campuses, or "Eastern elites." It's a gun-slinger's attitude toward ideas of "shoot first and ask questions later." It disparages our educational system with one-liners like "those who can, do, and those who can't, teach!" And today, while the internet makes some research much easier, it also offers an echo chamber for every type of paranoia.

Members of the "birther movement" never really wanted to know the truth. Rather, they wanted to plant doubt, to imply that Obama is not one of us, that he's a foreigner, an *Other* with a funny name and alien beliefs determined to take over *our* America. They couldn't be openly racist about the first black President, so they hit upon this tactic of asking *ad nauseum:* "Where was he born?" "No, where was he *really* born?"

Ambrose Bierce wrote, "Prejudice is a vagrant opinion without visible means of support." So if we want to fight back, we have to first admit that sometimes conspiracies are real: the plot to kill Lincoln, the Oklahoma City bombing, Al-Qaeda. We must learn to distinguish between competing ideas, without dismissing those we disagree with as baseless.

Feelings are not thoughts and thinking is hard work. Maturity is learning to live with ambiguity, to be able to acknowledge multiple opinions and choose reasonably among them. It's important to learn to question authority. But it's equally important to learn that you are entitled to your own opinions, but not to your own facts. Being able to distinguish between the two is ever more important in today's complex and contentious world.

The Downside of Ethanol

I've been trying to get my head around the ethanol or corn-as-fuel question and it's giving me a first-class headache. As a patriotic American, shouldn't I support any program that reduces our dependence on foreign oil controlled by ratty people like Hugo Chavez of Venezuela? By one optimistic estimate, if we put all our corn into fuel we could replace one quarter of our imported oil.

Shouldn't I rejoice that generous federal subsidies (my tax dollars) of fifty-one cents per gallon would spur the construction of scores more ethanol refineries across the country, adding jobs and wealth to local America?

Shouldn't I be happy that longtime subsidy skeptics Hillary Clinton and John McCain now agree on the need for such investment in the cause of energy independence? And as a Prius-driving environmentalist, don't I want further to reduce consumption of fossil fuels, and support these plucky Midwestern efforts to cut global warming? Well, sure!

But then suspicions, like methane-rich swamp gas, begin to waft into my nostrils. Maybe proponents of this new fuel suffer from what former Federal Reserve chair Alan Greenspan called an "irrational exuberance?" Using a life-cycle energy analysis, when you take all the money spent on the energy used to produce ethanol—that is, to build the machinery, make the fertilizer, run the tractors, transport the corn, burn the corn, transport the waste—the net energy gain is only about 15 percent.

Then, just maybe, Clinton and McCain didn't so much take the high-road of subsidies as the low road of electioneering as they pandered to voters in Iowa, which just happens to grow the most corn in the nation. This headlong rush to use food for fuel starts to smack of destroying the Alaskan National Wildlife Refuge to drill for a mere half-year's consumption of oil. According to Robbin Johnson, a former vice-president at Cargill Grain Company and University of Minnesota Professor C. Ford Runge, burning coal for energy independence is greenwash. Even if the entire U.S. corn crop were used to make ethanol, it would displace less gasoline usage than raising fleet fuel economy standards five miles per gallon, something readily achievable with existing technologies.

Now consider how this ethanol craze has helped drive up world prices for corn and other food grains such as wheat and barley. *The Economist* magazine points out that while we spend about one-tenth of our income on food, in the poorest countries it can be more than 50 percent. Last year, Mexicans rioted over the doubling in price of their corn-based tortillas. For them tortillas are staples, not snack food.

To me, it's not just ironic that our proclaimed environmentalism on replacing fossil fuels could speed starvation for the world's poor and further damage the world eco-systems—it's immoral.

Re-set in the Middle East

I majored in Middle East history in college. Admittedly, that was fifty years ago, but unfortunately, while much has changed in the ensuing years, much has remained the same. My most influential teacher was Professor William Polk, whose book, *Backdrop to Tragedy*, looked at the origins of Israeli-Palestine conflict from three perspectives: that of a Palestinian Arab, an Israeli Jew, and his own. He taught our small seminar that in a region where politics could be summed up as God, blood, and oil, we should always suspect absolutes and easy truths.

He also said that when we set out to define America's national interests in the Middle East, our guiding principle should be similar to that offered by Lord Palmerston for nineteenth century Great Britain: "We have neither eternal allies nor eternal enemies, only eternal and perpetual interests to whom we owe our duty."

I thought of this as I listened to President Obama's intelligent, subtle, and stirring speech at Cairo University last week. The mind boggles at the various audiences he was addressing: university students, Arab moderates, Arab radicals, Iranians, Iraqis, Sunnis, Shia, Afghans, Turks, Syrians, Pakistanis, the Taliban, Jews in Israel, Jews outside of Israel, Muslims in the U.S., and the rest of us bystanders. He talked comfortably about religion without self-righteousness or embarrassment. And he didn't pander to a domestic hard-line religious constituency.

The tone was knowledgeable, not pedantic; it was humble, not obsequious. In a forthright manner, he said, "Freedom in America is indivisible from the freedom to practice one's religion." In a region where words are parsed like Biblical text, Obama was unafraid to use terms like "colonialism" and "occupation." Cleverly, his "enemies" list was narrowly focused upon Al-Qaeda, thus avoiding the stereotypical confluence of Muslim and terrorism. Indeed, the words "terror" and "terrorist" were totally absent from his fifty-five minute speech.

He said that American support of Israel was unbreakable, but that "the position of the Palestinian people is intolerable. Americans will not turn our backs on the legitimate Palestinian aspirations for dignity, opportunity, and a state of their own." He told the Israelis to stop slicing and dicing the West Bank into protected Israeli settlements that make a two-state solution impossible.

Obama also understands the fundamental struggle within Islam to find a balance between the secular and the religious, to explore the reach of so-called "political Islam," and to determine whether there can be a viable separation of mosque and state. My only quibble is that he didn't get to the oil part, and how our dependence on Middle East oil has made us into hypocrites. We support dictatorial regimes who govern against our ideals because we want the oil. But maybe that's a subject for a future speech.

In the meantime, I agree with former diplomat Charles Freeman, who called this new formulation of American Middle East policy, "the mother of all re-sets."

Niebuhr and Obama

After President Obama's Nobel Prize acceptance speech, a number of observers remarked that it sounded like a sermon by Reinhold Niebuhr. I agreed, but I was not surprised. In fact, it was Obama's compelling summation of Niebuhr's philosophy in the spring of 2007 that made me an early supporter of his candidacy.

Reinhold Niebuhr was a preacher, theologian, political philosopher, and gadfly to true believers of all faiths and doctrines. Claimed by both conservatives and liberals, he had an extraordinary influence on American public discourse from the 1930s to the 1960s. What gave him such authority was his ability to write and preach about the tragedy of life, the irony of history, and the fallibility of human beings. He considered Lincoln the ideal statesman, because he combined "moral resoluteness about the immediate issues with a religious awareness of another dimension of meaning."

Obama's synopsis of Niebuhr went this way: "There's serious evil in the world, and hardship and pain. And we should be humble and modest in our belief we can eliminate those things. But we shouldn't use that as an excuse for cynicism and inaction. I take away...the sense we have to make these efforts knowing they are hard, and not swinging from naïve idealism to bitter realism."

You might say I got Niebuhr with my mother's milk, for during the year after I was born; she worked with Niebuhr and a group of other interventionists to awake an isolationist America to the Nazi threat when Great Britain stood alone.

During the Cold War, Niebuhr fought the Soviets with equal vigor. But beware, he cautioned his countrymen, "We must fight their falsehood with our truth, but we must also fight the falsehood in our own truth." And in the sixties, he broke with his dear friend Hubert Humphrey in his opposition to the Vietnam war.

In college I read a number of his books and heard him preach. I even met him several times when he was in residence for a semester and he and his wife used to give teas to the curious and the devout. Niebuhr coined masterly aphorisms; I posted my favorite one on the wall of my classroom. "Man's capacity for justice makes democracy possible, but man's capacity for injustice makes democracy necessary."

I read Obama's Oslo speech with a signed photograph of Niebuhr looking down from my study wall. "I face the world as it is," Obama said, "and cannot stand idle in the face of threats to the American people. Evil does exist in the world. A nonviolent movement could not have halted Hitler's armies. Negotiations cannot convince Al-Qaeda's leaders to lay down their arms. To say that force is sometimes necessary is not a call to cynicism—it is a recognition of history, the imperfections of man and the limits of reason."

It's a tribute to Niebuhr's complexity that I'm unsure of just how he would respond to Obama's characterization of Afghanistan as a "just war."

Putting a Country in a Corner

L ast month, President Obama called for a "reset" to our tattered relations with Russia. But then, in a *Wall Street Journal* interview, vice president Joseph Biden was as hawkish and critical of the Russians as Dick Cheney ever was. Among other things, he said, "The Russians have a shrinking population base, they have a withering economy, they have a banking sector and structure that is not likely to be able to withstand the next fifteen years, they're in a situation where the world is changing before them and they're clinging to something in the past that is not sustainable." He went on, "It's in their overwhelming military interest to reduce the number of nuclear weapons. All of a sudden, did they have an epiphany and say, 'Hey man, we don't want to threaten our neighbors?' No. They can't sustain it. Does that mean they won't do something stupid? No."

The *Wall Street Journal* (WSJ) editors loved it, but the Russians were incensed by his hectoring, patronizing tone. I wondered why Biden would say such things. Perhaps he and Obama are doing some king of good cop/bad cop routine. Or maybe the administration has decided that our positions are irredeemably opposed and we neither need nor expect Russian cooperation on a variety of foreign policy issues?

Or, maybe, since Biden has long been known for his runaway tongue, this was just Ole Joe Biden running his mouth again, and no one should take him seriously. Well, he is the vice president, and the Russians do take remarks like this quite seriously. As an autocratic, nuclear-armed state with a thousand year history of geo-political paranoia, it's understandable that they should wonder who is speaking.

The last I knew, we wanted their help to restrain North Korea from further nuclear threats, to reduce nuclear weapons, to improve supplies to Afghanistan, to prevent Iran from getting a bomb, and for moderating the Palestine-Israel conflict—all laudable objectives. But at the same time, we have kept pushing NATO eastward right into Ukraine and Georgia, virtually Russia's backyard. We have pushed for an anti-missile system in Eastern Europe, against Iran, also into what Russia calls its historic sphere of influence.

We deny that sphere-of-influence theory. But unfortunately, the Russians have a lot more ways to pressure us than we do them. Examples include a veto in the Security Council, naval exercises in the Caribbean, lack of help with Iran and North Korea, and increased pressure on the natural gas pipelines to Europe. I think (and fervently hope) that Biden himself may have recognized this when he said later in the WSJ interview, "It is never smart to embarrass an individual or a country when they're dealing with significant loss of face. My dad used to put it another way: "Never put another man in a corner where the only way out is over you. It just is not smart."

Thinking about the Past
Learning about the Future

From Sword to Plow

On the city green in Westfield, Massachusetts stands a statue of a Revolutionary War-era figure in a three-cornered hat and cape, with a rocky jaw, which looks strikingly like George Washington. This is actually my maternal great-great-great-great-great grandfather General William Lyman Shepard. He had two careers: farming and war. At the age of sixteen, he enlisted in the British army and fought through the entire French and Indian War.

He returned to Westfield and farmed for the next ten years until, in 1774, he joined the Committees of Correspondence, a proto-Revolutionary group of postal conspirators who collected grievances against the British king. At the Battle of Boston he was made a colonel of the Massachusetts militia. At the battle of Long Island, his troops protected Washington's escape to New Jersey; in that battle he was shot through the neck. As he was borne from the field, he asked for water. When he found he could drink, he told the surgeon, "I'm all right, doctor! Stick on a plaster and tie on my cravat, for I am going out again." And he did.

He fought at Trenton, Princeton, and Saratoga. Overall, he survived twenty-two battles and the grueling winter at Valley Forge. After the war, he went back to farming. He also served on the Massachusetts Governor's Council, was an elector in the first two presidential races, served three terms in Congress, and was one of the councilors appointed to write treaties with the Penobscot Indians and Six Nations confederation. He died at the then-uncommon age of eighty.

In our family he is famous not just for his military exploits, but for the angry and anguished letter he sent from the misery of Valley Forge to the members of the Massachusetts legislature in comfortable and safe Boston. He wrote the state had not provided the troops with any material support for more than three months. There were, he said, "at least four hundred men in the Brigade which I belong to that have not a shoe nor a stocking to put on and more than that number have not half a shirt apiece...I have seen soldiers turned out to do their duty in such poor condition that notwithstanding all the hard heartedness I am naturally possessed of, I could not refrain from tears. It would melt the heart of a savage to see the state we are in."

There is no record that any shoes came.

This Thanksgiving, as detachments of the Vermont National Guard begin returning home from deployment to Afghanistan and Iraq, I'll be reminded of General Shepard's story, 220 years after he, too, lay down his sword and returned to the plow.

Remembering Charlie Houston

One endearing thing about Charlie Houston, a world-renowned mountain climber and medical researcher who died this week at the age of ninety-six, was that you had to do your own research to learn about his life. He never volunteered much about his accomplishments. He wasn't falsely modest. He was just more interested in the future than in the past.

So where to start? Well, I went to Wikipedia first.

In spare prose, it describes him as an "American physician, mountaineer, high-altitude investigator, inventor, author, film-maker, former Peace Corps administrator, and participant in important and celebrated attempts to climb the Himalayan mountain K2."

Charlie began climbing at the age of twelve. By the time he was a senior in college he had participated in the ascent of Nanda Devi, the tallest mountain climbed until then. During World War II, Charlie's studies of altitude tolerance helped the Allied pilots to defeat Japanese and German flyers. After the war his research included ground-breaking work on pulmonary edema and retinal hemorrhages. In the early 1960s he led the Peace Corps in India. When Peace Corps Director Bill Moyers became deathly ill on a visit to India, Charlie saved his life and they became lifelong friends.

Charlie wrote five books about his climbing and altitude research, but the title of Bernadette MacDonald's biography captured his essence in a cherished phrase to describe mountaineering: *Brotherhood of the Rope.* According to Geoff Tabin, an ophthalmologist who climbed Mt. Everest in 1983, "In the 1930s Charlie was a quiet visionary of organization and technique in mountain exploration. In his later years, when climbing had become a huge industry, Charlie was the curmudgeonly keeper of the morals of mountaineering."

For forty years the Houston home on Ledge Road in Burlington was a Grand Central Station of visitors from around town and around the world who came for free and spirited enquiry into the human experience. At the same time, Charlie also loved his gardens, and as Moyers said about him in a TV special, he never failed to fill the bird feeders.

Charlie's curiosity was limitless. He followed the news closely, even after his sight dimmed. He would plump you down in a comfortable chair before a big picture window that looked out over Lake Champlain. With his beloved golden retriever Pooh-bear at his feet, he'd ask eagerly, "What are you doing? " What do you think about this?" Then you'd move on to politics, history, science, and medicine. He had plenty of very strong opinions on certain subjects, like public health, but he would consider other points of view if arguments were persuasive.

As he went blind, a "brotherhood" of readers developed who rotated through to read and discuss with him books of all types and length. Charlie Houston was trained to treat people's physical illnesses. But to his final days, his special "brotherhood of the mind" helped maintain the intellectual vitality of hundreds of his admirers.

Inspired by Thesiger

The recent death of Sir Edmund Hillary reminds me—also a writer, former teacher, and legislator—of another explorer who fired my imagination as a young man.

I was never a climber. The highest I ever got was fifteen thousand feet up Mount Kenya, above which the technical ascent began. The only passion I shared with Hillary was beekeeping. The Hillary of *my* dreams was an intrepid wanderer named Sir Wilfred Thesiger, who died in 2003 at the age of ninety-two. While studying Middle Eastern history in college, I became fascinated with a cadre of eccentric English explorers who challenged themselves and the deserts of Saudi Arabia: St. John Philby, Bertram Thomas, Henry Doughty, T.E. Lawrence, and Thesiger.

Born to a comfortable life as the son of the British minister to the Ethiopian court, Thesiger was educated at Oxford, after which he mounted original expeditions in Darfur and eastern Ethiopia in his twenties. After service in World War II, when he won Britain's second highest military decoration for bravery, he returned to his life's passion for exploration. During forty-five years he walked over forty thousand miles in Africa, Arabia, Iraq, and Afghanistan, seeking out one remote tribe after another to share their lives and privations. He was also a marvelous photographer whose powerful black and white images are a striking addition to the four books he wrote.

When William Polk, one of my college professors, invited me to join him and four Bedouins as the journey's photographer on a twelve hundred mile camel trek from Riyadh, Saudi Arabia to Amman, Jordan, I jumped at the chance. For inspiration, I took along Thesiger's book "Arabian Sands," an account of his trek across the forbidding Empty Quarter of southern Saudi Arabia. Our journey in the northern Arabian desert had its share of adventures—getting lost, running out of water, and the like—but they were mouse meat compared to the hardships and dangers Thesiger endured in the Empty Quarter.

Indeed, in all his travels, Thesiger pushed the world's physical and ethnographic boundaries as he pushed his body to its limits. He was a man of extreme austerity, wrote one obituary. "The harder a journey was—extreme shortages of food and water, hostility of terrain and weather—the more he enjoyed it." But as with all of us, he had contrasting sides to his personality. In writings and interviews, he bemoaned the softening effects settled civilization brought to the nomads he ennobled in words and photos, but when I met him in London for tea he was dressed in a three-piece suit and, but for his world-weathered face, looked like any anonymous civil servant.

At the end of our desert journey, Bill Polk and I had a similar sharp jab of cultural contrast. While we congratulated ourselves for surviving the first trek of Westerners across the great Nefud in one hundred years, one of our Arab companions dryly remarked, "It would have been more comfortable in a truck."

Reclaiming the Twin Towers

On the anniversary of 9/11, we steel ourselves for another somber flood of memorials, cries of "Never again!" and speeches at Ground Zero. However, an antidote to such gloom comes in a film that recaptures the moment, twenty-seven years prior to 9/11, of one man's riveting and peaceful conquest of that same Manhattan airspace.

Now I know this kind of stunt is against the law for essentially good reasons, but the juxtaposition of these two events is at the transcendent heart of the film "Man On Wire," a brilliant and high-charged docudrama about Phillip Petit's epochal tightrope walk between the World Trade Towers in August 1974.

Nowhere in the film is there a single reference to, or image of, the rain of death, destruction, and horror of September 11, 2001. Yet you cannot watch those tell-tale steel facades, figuratively travel the elevators, escalators and stairs, or see crowds of puzzled anxious faces looking skyward without thinking of that black day.

Director James Marsh shrewdly lets the viewer complete this documentary with his own memories. His laser focus is upon the irrepressible Petit, who seemed to be painting the air with his twenty-foot balancing pole. Marsh shows the trajectory of Petit's mission through a tightly-wrought mix of present-day interviews with Petit and his Franco-American team of co-conspirators, film footage from the preparations for the actual event, and some clever re-enactments to fill in the gaps.

As the film unfolds, you see the depth of Petit's dual rebellion against authority and gravity, and his fixation to bridge improbable spaces. Although his training in the French and American countrysides, recorded in grainy '70s home video, has some of the mad-cap quality of a Beatles film, you also see the care with which he used practical physics to rig his cables and ropes. His prior aerial triumphs, the twin towers of Notre Dame (during a Mass, no less), and a harbor bridge in Sydney, Australia prepared him (and now you) for the main event.

You learn how he assembled his team, human filings drawn to his magnetic dream. They were like a team of bank robbers whose preparations, arguments, and audacity reminded me of the jewel burglary in the classic French film "Rififi." Petit was like an aerial Willy Sutton, who, when asked why he did this, said it's because that's where the space was and the performance.

A special note of praise goes to the music, mostly by Michael Nyman, an English composer, which fits the caper like a glove. It is by turns sublime, spooky, affectionate, never intrusive, and always supportive. It climaxes with Erik Satie's "Gymnopedies," roughly translated as poetic gymnastics, a perfect match for Petit's giddy performance.

Petit was a burglar of sorts, stealing our hearts and breath in his victory of daring and spirit. But with the experience he stole atop those now-iconic towers, he also gave back to the world, making our memory of them triumphantly whole once more—at least for ninety minutes in a darkened theater.

Coolidge on Fishing

As fishing season opens, it's a good time to remember that President Calvin Coolidge had some memorable fishing adventures during his five years in the White House. Today it's inconceivable that a president could take months for vacation, yet in the summers of 1926, '27 and '28, Coolidge left Washington for stays of six weeks, two months, and almost three months in the Adirondacks, the Black Hills of South Dakota, and the Brule River in northern Wisconsin.

Although Coolidge had been only a desultory angler as a boy, his Secret Service chief Edmund Starling vowed to teach him fishing in general and fly-fishing in particular. In the lures he chose, Coolidge was no elitist, using both worms and flies. Moreover, he lived up to his waste-not/want-not reputation. Once on the Brule River, he asked the guide if he should use a sinker. No, he was told, the weight of the worm will keep the hook down.

"Well, then shall I use the whole worm or break it in half?"

"Oh, put on the whole worm," the guide said, "and make sure the ends wiggle."

Even in Coolidge's day, the inclination of fishermen to lie was widely known. As a fishing politician, he was doubly suspect. Therefore, when he caught seven trout in the Black Hills one day, he displayed them proudly because, as the *New York Times* reported, "scarcely anyone believes a fisherman and the president therefore thinks it is wise to produce the actual evidence."

However, while researching my book about presidential fishing, I heard a different tale. In West Yellowstone, Wyoming, I talked to Wally Eagle, whose family has owned an outfitting store there for eighty years. In the summer of 1927, his father was fishing near the president's party in Yellowstone Park. Wally's dad had caught a mess of trout, but when he asked one of the president's guides about the First Angler's luck, he learned that the president was skunked. So he gave the guide a few of his trout for the president. Later in the day, after Coolidge had given a speech at the Old Faithful Inn, he was asked, "How was the fishing?"

"Well," said the president, "I have always heard that you judge a

94

fisherman by the contents of his creel." Thereupon he displayed the shimmering fish to his audience. As Wally Eagle remarked, "No one ever asked the president if *he* caught the fish!"

Political cartoonists love to use non-political activities to illustrate political events, so when Coolidge opted out of the 1928 presidential campaign, *Washington Star* cartoonist Clifford Berryman drew Coolidge in a Chippewa canoe with a fishing pole at the ready, saying, "Choosin' to run isn't as restful as this."

Coolidge knew that his fishing enthusiasm exceeded his ability. But he still longed for membership in the fraternity. During his stay in Wisconsin, Coolidge once lost a fish. As Starling wrote, "I heard the president say 'Damn!' Then he turned to me and with a shy smile, said, 'Guess I'm a real fisherman now. I cussed.'"

Tipping and Turning

For my "turning point," I chose the "tipping point," the name of Malcolm Gladwell's book of several years back. Gladwell took the folk cliché of "the straw that broke the camel's back" and turned it into a best seller. Clever him!

The tipping point is the point of critical mass, the threshold, the boiling point, the match at the powder keg, when long gestating quantitative change explodes into qualitative change. It's the moment when *evolution* becomes *revolution*. Gladwell's case studies range from enquiring into why Paul Revere was effective in arousing the colonists, but fellow rider William Dawes was not, to why Hush Puppies' shoes caught on.

To the straw and camel metaphor, Gladwell added actors of his own naming. Three groups of individuals are decisive in tipping the balance in favor of new ideas. They are the Mavens, who are alert for novelty, the Connectors, who pass on the idea to others, and the Salesmen, who sell the idea to the general public. I began applying the idea to other cases in weather, politics, diseases, human motivation, and fashion. When does purple become blue? When does a person become gray-haired or get the flu or become bearded? When does a sky turn cloudy or annoyance become anger?

Besides being the object of these semantic games, the phrase has joined a few other useful phrases in my analytical knapsack. "Only connect!" Those two words near the end of E.M. Forster's novel *Howard's End* have resonated for me for thirty years as a useful mantra to simplify both teaching and learning. In a college class called "The Enterprise of Science," chemist Leonard Nash explained the scientific method to us non-scientists that science wasn't so much about finding something utterly new as it was looking at the same information in a new way. "Putting on a new thinking cap," he said, in words a second-grader could understand.

So I tip my cap to the "tipping point" and to other useful clichés.

Reconciling Our World
with Our Community

One Beehive at a Time

Since 2005, I have gone to Central America at least once a year to study Spanish, be a casual tourist, and do some volunteer work with beekeepers. Each year I see new places and my linguistic comfort zone extends farther from the classroom and restaurant to the store, the street, and the bus. Most importantly, it now reaches into the countryside where the bees are located.

I've worked hard to gain fluency in the specialized vocabulary of beekeeping, so that while I can't talk much politics with *campesinos*, I can sure talk beekeeping. Our discussions are mainly about organizational structure, techniques, and marketing. My guiding principle has been to pose lots of questions and only volunteer an opinion when asked. I'm on familiar ground in discussing diseases, bee temperament, and how to sell honey locally.

The clearest difference lies in business organization. Most of these guys (and almost all are men) belong to democratically-run cooperatives, often involving hundreds of members, with a tradition going back to pre-Columbian times. The U.S. has only one honey cooperative, the Sioux Bee Association that produces about 20 percent of all American commercial honey. All the rest of our honey comes from individual beekeepers.

I find it both surprising and satisfying to compare practices from region to region. Having visited seven different beekeeping operations in four countries, I've become a sort of human Google, passing on ideas about U.S. practices of course, but also sharing experiences between beekeepers in Mexico, Guatemala, Panama, and Nicaragua.

I couldn't help the individual beekeeper calculate the best use of his time between honey and coffee production and his own subsistence plot of corn and beans. But I could assist the cooperatives to think through their local, regional, and international marketing plan. My biggest satisfaction was hatching a plan to bring Mexican master beekeepers to Nicaragua to launch a beekeeping training program.

Much as I enjoy the work, there's another reason I make these trips. I feel guilty about U.S. policies concerning this region over the last 150 years. From gunboat diplomacy and taking the Panama Canal to desta-bilizing governments in Guatemala, Chile, and Nicaragua all in the name of free trade, the Monroe Doctrine, and anti-Communism, the U.S. has a lot to answer for. What did Porforio Diaz, the Mexican leader say? "Poor Mexico, so far from God, so near to the United States."

I think it's particularly ironic that if we hadn't taken New Mexico, Arizona, much of Colorado, Utah, and California from Mexico in 1848, Mexico would be a much richer country and far fewer of its people would need to emigrate, illegally or otherwise.

So now I do what I can to make amends: one man, one conversation, one beehive at a time.

Friends

After seeing the film *The Social Network*, and reading that Facebook, the subject of the film, has more than five hundred million "friends," I began to muse about the nature of friendship. Just what is a friend, I wondered.

Settling on a definition turned out to be harder than I thought. There's an Amazon-wide spectrum of "friends" based upon shared activities, agreeable temperaments, and pure happenstance. From drinking buddies to foxhole buddies. From teammates to seatmates. From a TV sitcom to a pacifist sect. There are political friends of Bill Clinton and friends of George Bush who just raise money.

Someone, maybe Groucho Marx, joked that the difference between a friend and an old friend is five minutes. Facebook has shortened that to a few keystrokes, while at the same time turning the noun "friend" into a verb. Early last month, Mark Zuckerberg, the founder of Facebook, announced a completely overhauled, brand-new version of Facebook Groups. He said, "It's a simple way to stay up-to-date with small groups of your friends and to share things with only them. The default setting is Closed, which means only members see what's going on in a group. The net effect is your whole experience is organized around spaces of the people you care most about."

Well, gosh, I say, that sounds like the privacy and control we had before Facebook came on the scene. Even the social network recognizes that one "friend" does not fit all. Personally, I would define good friends as people who inspire me, stimulate me, get me out of myself, and accept my weaknesses, like my good friend the late Bill Gray, who once said that a true friend would drop everything to answer your call for help, no questions asked.

Indeed, as Cicero said, "A friend is, as it were, a second self." When we're seized by the urge to blog, to tweet, to re-work our Facebook page, aren't we really doing this for ourselves, not for these digital friends? Friendship is a complex relationship, not just a touch-and go landing. Another friend, who has lived in both rural Vermont and bustling Burlington, observed that small town friendships were fewer but more broad-ranging, while those in Burlington were more numerous, but shallower.

When it comes to having many friends, I like to think of the Olympic symbol of over-lapping intertwined rings: circles of neighbors, college chums, family, other volunteer workers, book club members, fellow teachers, legislators, running buddies, on and on. The more they overlap, the closer the friendship. Henry Adams, the descendant of two presidents—John Adams and John Quincy—wrote, "One friend in a lifetime is much; two are many; three are hardly possible. Friendship needs a certain parallelism of life, a community of thought, a rivalry of aim."

Come to think of it, he could have been writing about the person who's been my best friend (without the assistance of Facebook) for more than forty years. And that person is my wife.

How Do We Get the News?

On a recent Sunday, the *New York Times* ran a piece about the rise of non-professional journalism. The most notorious—some would say enterprising—example of this trend was a woman's secret recording of Barack Obama's description of rural Pennsylvania voters as clinging to "guns and religion."

That same Sunday, while cleaning files in my home office, I found some clippings of stories I'd written as a reporter for the *Burlington Free Press* thirty years ago. Holding those brown bits of paper, I reflected upon how much journalism has changed since those glory days of the late 1970s. It was only a few years after Watergate, and journalism schools were filling up like recruiting stations after Pearl Harbor. In my ten-year journalism career with four different newspapers, I was trained to dig for stories, to look for multiple points of view, to be respectful and protective of sources, and to keep my opinions out of my reporting.

Today, an ever-growing class of non-professional or "alternative" journalists scorns objectivity as a false creed. Jane Hamsher, who runs a political web site called Firedoglake, told the *Times*, "Journalists should be loyal to their readers, not to their subjects." She exemplifies what former Vermonter Dan Gillmor described in his book *We the Media*: citizen journalists who turn news from a lecture into a conversation.

Over those thirty years, the gap between news and entertainment narrowed both in ownership and in presentation. Talk radio became ubiquitous. National and state public radio stations came into being. Reporting scandals at the *New York Times* and *Washington Post* tarnished their revered authority. Reality television gave us a new oxymoron. And many young people, like our twenty-something sons, found Comedy Central more credible than network news.

The greatest change was, of course, the internet, which now provides instant access not only to stalwarts like the BBC and CNN, but also to all the newspapers and news services we'll ever want to read. It also brings discussion groups, neighborhood bulletin boards, and the multifarious clipping services of our friends.

The web's extraordinary search capacity has allowed more of us to do our own digging and reporting. YouTube and blogs are also building a digital Information Mall of the World, full of self, stupidity, sham, and significance.

This profusion of news has spawned one immense unintended consequence. Under the new journalistic rules, there are no rules, no gatekeepers, and no editors. As the web drenches us with individual prejudices and preconceptions of every shade and stripe, it becomes a tempting echo chamber for our own views. This poses a greater burden on ordinary citizens to separate the wheat from the chaff...and not keep the chaff.

So it would seem that even with new journalism, one fundamental thing remains the same: the citizen's responsibility to evaluate all this new information and then act—do something constructive with it—the better to contribute to a democratic society.

Getting What We Pay For

In 1900, when the press barons William R. Hearst and Joseph Pulitzer were battling each other over newspaper circulation and New York City had fifteen dailies, *The Atlantic Monthly* magazine observed, "The two cardinal responsibilities of the literary life in the newspaper day are namely crowding eternity into five minutes (and then) getting anyone to take five minutes to notice that eternity."

But if newspaper publishing was challenging back then, it is even more so now, with far more competition for reader attention and dollars. The last few years have been locust years for newspapers. Some, like the *Rocky Mountain News* in Denver, have simply disappeared. Others have cut staff down to the bone and beyond. The venerable *Christian Science Monitor* has gone digital, while headlines and photos have grown larger, in papers ranging from regionals such as the *Burlington Free Press* to giants like the *New York Times*.

Other forces are at work here, too: a rotten economy, the flight of big advertising revenue for cars, housing, and personals, to free sites like Craigslist, the rise of weeklies, and new electronic venues like the *Front Page Forum* in Burlington.

Then there are the changing public attitudes. Some people say, Why should we care about newspapers, this print version of the sometimes-scorned mainstream media? We have YouTube. We have Facebook. We have our own blogs or those of others who agree with us. And if we need to know any news, we'll get it off the internet, for free.

This kind of remark makes Chuck Lewis, an old reporter friend of mine from Chicago, apoplectic. (He happens to be Washington bureau chief of the Hearst Newspaper chain.) He points out that the so-called free news people get off the internet most likely comes by way of links to the much maligned mainstream media—that same mainstream media that financially supports the journalistic efforts of the ground troops of journalism: reporters. These reporters write the first drafts of history, telling both sides of the story.

Newspapers are at the top of the print-news chain, making the financial investments those internet news efforts—especially bloggers—depend on and frequently exploit. The fallacy that online news is free undermines not only the journalism business, but our civic fabric as well. If no one will pay a reporter to sit through the local zoning board hearing, how will we know who voted to allow the building height variance, and why?

As James Surowiecki wrote recently in *The New Yorker* magazine, "For a while now, readers have had the best of both worlds: all the benefits of the old, high-profit regime—intensive reporting, experienced editors, and so on—and the low costs of the new one. But that situation can't last. Soon enough, we're going to start getting what we pay for, and we may find out just how little that is. "

Two Servings of the Same Dish

As President Obama was signing the law to expand national volunteer programs, I was working as a volunteer teaching beekeeping and English in a rural school in Patagonia, Argentina. Compare their one inhabitant per square mile with Vermont's sixty per square mile, and you can see that it's decidedly rural.

The rugged landscape looks like parts of our Wild West at the time of Butch Cassidy and the Sundance Kid—who actually hid here for a couple of years before the final shoot-out in Bolivia. You could make Westerns in Patagonia 'til the cows came home. The boarding school where I taught was founded twenty-five years ago by idealistic university graduates from Buenos Aires, who came to this remote region to teach Mapuche Indian children living in communities up to three hundred miles away. The school now has about two hundred students, one third of them girls. From the beginning, the school's founders and teachers wove together academic and tech-ed tracks.

To a traditional curriculum of history, English, math, computing and so on, they graft one that includes agro-technical courses such as forestation, beekeeping, vegetable gardens, animal husbandry, carpentry, and basic electricity. Thus, upon graduation, the young men and women can choose whether to go back to the countryside, move into the job market, or even go to a university. As of last year, 95 percent of the graduates either got jobs or went on to some kind of college.

The school raises most of its own meat, vegetables, and fruits, while students do most of the manual labor around the campus. In addition, the school annually sells about $30,000 worth of preserves, vegetables, eggs, and honey in local markets. Ten years after building the school, the founders realized that their mission was more than education; it had to include economic development in these impoverished regions to help provide jobs the graduates could return to. Thus, students and teachers now do traineeships in their home communities in such activities as electrical wiring, green house construction, and honey production.

One day I accompanied a pair of teachers on a one hundred mile dirt road trip to sell wool from the school's sheep and llamas to women in the country. They would then make cloth and rugs to sell in artisan outlets in the cities. From the beginning, the school has welcomed volunteers with almost any talent, or even just muscle. Last year, nearly 350 volunteers came from Argentina and ten other countries.

During my stay, the school hosted a theater director, a Dutch graduate student studying community development, a weaver, myself, and twenty-five high school students from Buenos Aires to work on the farm. Then it hit me. This dish of collective action between students, teachers, parents, and volunteers had a familiar taste. The proportions and spices were different, but I realized we had served this dish at Champlain Valley Union High School, where I taught, and in a host of other activities in Vermont. Together, these people were, in the words of the CVU mission statement, "contributing members of a democratic society."

Fast Food, Fast Eating

I've filled the car with gas; now I'm filling my own stomach. I'm sitting in the parking lot of a convenience store in Burlington, reading the *New York Times* and making cell phone calls while I wolf down a cheeseburger, a candy bar, and a cup of lukewarm coffee.

The hamburger tastes like low-grade cardboard and the cheese like kindergarten paste. No matter. I'm multi-tasking, that widely practiced technique which connotes efficiency, but often just means *busy-ness*.

My eyes scroll down the business page to a headline that makes me do a double-take: "Eat Quickly, for the Economy's Sake." It's a column by Floyd Norris that reports on a survey by the Organization of Economic Cooperation and Development about the living conditions of their members. It suggests that nations where people eat faster have higher rates of growth in their gross domestic product. The dividing line between the fast eaters and slow eaters is one hundred minutes for meals per day, the survey said.

Norris is quick to say that this correlation is not to be confused with causation. We don't know, for example, if people spend more time at meals because they have less to do when economies are not growing, or if economies slow down because citizens are dawdling over second cups of coffee or glasses of wine when they should be at work. The report makes another cautious correlation between economic growth and obesity. Some of the less obese countries—France, South Korea, Japan, Italy and Norway—grew more slowly that the more obese: U.S. Mexico, Britain, Australia and New Zealand.

"Hmmmm," I think. When my wife isn't home, it probably takes me less than minutes a day to chow down on bagels, soup, apples, honey, peanut butter, salads and cheddar cheese, as well as my share of ice cream and donuts. At that speed, I could almost call my eating patriotic, like following President Bush's injunction after the 9/11 attack to go shopping.

Plus, I'm among the lucky ones who have dodged the obesity bullet. My weight hasn't varied more than five pounds in fifty years, except when I'm sick. The trouble is that eating on the run still leads to indigestion, which leads me to think about the Slow Food Movement. That's a twenty-year-old world-wide crusade with over one hundred thousand members. They hate everything about fast food, from its preparation to its consumption. Here is part of their manifesto:"We are enslaved by speed and have all succumbed to the same insidious virus: fast life, which disrupts our habits, pervades the privacy of our homes and forces us to eat fast foods." And, "fast life has changed our way of being, and threatens our environment and our landscapes. So slow food is now the only truly progressive answer."

Now, I'll agree that's a bit pretentious, but the idea that we make a positive contribution to the gross domestic product through bad eating habits sounds to me, well, kind of gross. Guess I'll have to re-think my taste for fast food and fast eating.

Teaching about Bees, Learning about Life

I just spent two weeks in southern Mexico working on a project to teach coffee farmers how to keep bees. Our object is to help reduce their economic dependence upon coffee, whose widely fluctuating world price is beyond their control. For three years, I picked away at this idea on my own. This year, I persuaded Professor Dewey Caron, a leading beekeeping scientist and teacher, to go along with me. Born and raised in Vermont, with a UVM degree, Dewey has spent forty years teaching beekeeping in the U.S. and in a dozen Latin American countries. Among his books is one about killer bees. Best of all, he's fluent in Spanish.

Honey has a long tradition as a natural sweetener in Central America. But twenty years ago, when the killer bees swept through the region, traditional or rustic beekeeping collapsed and honey production disappeared. Recently, however, pent-up demand and a readiness to use modern methods with the ubiquitous killer bees have brought back commercial honey production.

Our project is to write a three-section manual of best practices in beekeeping. One part deals with technical matters, such as producing one's own equipment or queen bees. The second section covers organizational challenges such as cooperative governance, the relationship between coffee and honey production, and the distribution of income among members. The final section treats honey marketing. For example, how might the cooperative brand its products, or spread its focus between local, national and international markets?

In discussions with managers and farmers across the region, we confirmed our pre-conception that none of the beekeepers were hobbyists as many are in the U.S.; they all wanted to produce honey for real income. We also made several counterintuitive discoveries. Several cooperatives, for example, chose not to sell their honey for the highest (Fair Trade, organic) prices, because they can sell everything they produce in the village markets.

In these two weeks, several experiences stood out:

We watched Alfredo Contreras, a second-generation beekeeper in

Oaxaca, Mexico with an extraordinary hive-side manner, as he taught the craft to young and old. He was passionately committed to empowering women who have long been marginalized from primary economic activities.

In Chiapas we met coffee farmers who had formed their cooperative after a 1997 massacre of members of a local civic organization who were named, ironically, Las Abejas, "The Bees."

In Nicaragua we saw Mexican beekeepers helping Nicaraguan coffee farmers set up their first honey cooperative.

These activities made this project particularly fulfilling, because Dewey and I were not gringos bringing tablets of wisdom and experience from afar, but rather gatherers and sharers of information. Everything in the final manual will be from the farmers themselves. When the trip ended, we came home fired up to work with our *own* bees. In Delaware, Dewey has no problem. My hives, however, are under a foot of snow.

It Pays to be Ignorant

I'm going to be a curmudgeon here.

Like all imperfect people, I've made countless stupid mistakes or otherwise embarrassed myself because I didn't know what was coming. However, the phrase "If I had only known" connotes regrets. It suggests that, through the rear-view mirror, knowledge is power or enlightenment. But there's another perspective from which to view the many moments that are the fruits of impulse, or come unbidden and unexpected. This is what I call "intelligent ignorance," because it's what you do with those surprises that makes life more interesting, challenging, and rewarding.

My own particular inverse square law posits that the more time I spend deciding something important, the worse is the final decision. My first three professional choices, which bore the stretch marks of months of cogitation, were total failures. Then, by chance, I fell into journalism. Of course, it *is* easier to contemplate the flameouts of long-past failures than to stare at the smoking wreckage of recent crashes.

But more times than I probably deserve, snap judgments have changed my life for the better. The best of them was falling in love with my wife in a Chicago elevator forty-one years ago. Thirty-eight years ago, on a lark, I took up beekeeping. It has been a lifelong passion. And it took me one second to decide to join the greatest physical adventure of my life, a twelve hundred mile camel trek across Saudi Arabia.

"If I had only known," life would have been a tamer, duller beast. In conclusion, I can't resist recalling a radio show of my youth called "It Pays to be Ignorant." With a panel of experts "who are dumber than you are, and can prove it," it parodied the high IQ shows like "Quiz Kids." The theme song went like this:

> It pays to be ignorant,
> to be dumb,
> to be dense,
> to be ignorant.
> It pays to be ignorant,
> Just like me.

What's the Dough Boy Afraid Of?

Back in the eighties, Pillsbury's Häagen-Dazs ice cream employed some hardball distribution tactics against Ben and Jerry's, who fought back with a clever series of ads asking, "What's the Dough Boy afraid of?"

One might ask a similar question about the fifty-year-old United States embargo on trade with Cuba. With the Cold War long over and Fidel Castro fading, what *is* Uncle Sam afraid of? Through ten presidents, we've been hoping to achieve regime change through economic strangulation. This has been U.S. policy since the failed Bay of Pigs invasion in 1961. Ironically, it was maintained by the influence of Cuban-American refugees who became a powerful force in Florida and American politics, and its continuation has been driven more by politics than by common sense.

Thanks to the embargo, the Cuban people are economically more miserable, though their sparse diets and arguably better overall health care have so far protected them from the epidemic of obesity that plagues other cultures, including ours. But politically they are no freer, and we have given the Castros a convenient scapegoat for all their political oppression and economic mismanagement.

We have also continued to trade with regimes just as repressive as Cuba. China comes to mind. The embargo was supposed to isolate Cubans from the rest of the world, but to a great extent, it has backfired. In the latest of seventeen successive U.N. General Assembly resolutions to lift the embargo, Washington could find only two allies to oppose it: Israel and Palau, a Pacific island with a population of twenty-one thousand.

Finally, however, some attitudes are changing. For example, Jorge Mas Santos, chair of the Cuban American National Foundation (CANF) has recently written that "U.S. policy towards Cuba is at best static and at worst counterproductive, a source of increasing frustration to many Cuban Americans." A Zogby poll last fall found that 60 percent of Americans believe that Washington should revise its policies towards Cuba.

And some sharp criticism of the embargo now comes from conservative businessmen. In the words of Tom Donohue, CEO of the U.S. Chamber of Commerce: "All you have to do is go over to Cuba and watch how the Spanish, the French, the Latin Americans and everybody else on the globe are building resorts or trying to invest, and we are sitting here with a fifty-year-old policy that doesn't work."

One of our sons works in Argentina, and he has suggested that another good reason for Obama and Congress to lift the embargo would be its effect on our relations with the rest of Latin America. Obama wouldn't need to tour the region. He could simply announce the economic version of troop withdrawal. It would be a cheap and brilliant way to sow goodwill among friends and confusion among enemies. This reminded me of something Mark Twain once wrote: "Do the right thing. It will gratify some people and astonish the rest."

Rationing Health Care

I've been thinking about the necessity of allocating scarce resources. The word for it is rationing—and it's a dirty word in the health care reform debate. But it shouldn't be. It's a fundamental part of any economic strategy, and anyone who thinks we have unlimited resources to spend on health care or anything else isn't being realistic.

As numerous economists have said, the U.S. spends far more on health care than other societies, but we get far less, and that means we're rationing badly. We'd rather promise everything to everybody, even though we know better. And if we were really honest, we'd admit that we already ration health care without calling it such. It's a kind of rationing when we, as individuals, short-change other expenses to pay for health care. And when companies are forced to pay more for employee health insurance policies, the result is that wages are rationed.

But pediatrician Joe Hagan, my good friend and running buddy, had some cautionary comments. "To put rationing at the core of health care reform seems an over-simplification. For example, overhead on insurance premiums is about 11 percent, for which we get no "health" value. The cost of processing claims for multiple insurance companies, each with an idiosyncratic way of doing business, is a small fortune in practice or hospital overhead. And as a nation—and this includes doctors—we often spend our health care dollars unwisely: little preventive care, little mental health care, lax safety standards. A case in point: why aren't bike helmets the law? They not only save lives, they save money!"

Okay, okay, Joe; I concede. Rationing is not the only solution, but it should still be in the calculus, because it brings a certain universal clarity to the debate. Here are some other bits of evidence: although the analogy is not exact, both the Department of Transportation and the Consumer Product Safety Commission make annual decisions based on how much we can reasonably invest in saving lives. And the British have determined that the public is willing to spend up to $49,000 to give a person an extra year of life.

One way to combine the economic, political, and ethical in making these difficult choices is by using a method called the QALY, or Quality Adjusted Life Year. For more than thirty years, it's helped us measure the cost-effectiveness of various medical procedures when the public foots the bill. Then there's the openly two-tiered system proposed by Princeton bioethicist Peter Singer. There would be a "Medicare for All." If you wanted to receive more treatments recommended by your own doctor, you could opt out of this program as long as you could demonstrate you had private resources when you fell ill. Or you could remain in it, and buy supplemental insurance.

As Singer writes, "Rationing explicitly, openly, honestly, means getting value for the billions we spend on health care. We have a right and duty to set limits on which treatments should be paid for out of the public purse."

Fair Trade is a Good Step

On my recent trips to Central America to work with coffee farmers and beekeepers, I've come to realize how difficult coffee production is, and how little farmers make from that $9.00 per pound or $2.50 per cappuccino we pay in the store and café. As those farmers begin planting next year's crop, which they will pick literally bean by bean, I've decided that I'm happy to pay a premium for my coffee, as long as most of that money gets back to the farmers who produced it.

That's where the concept of "fair trade" comes in. Fair trade advocates argue that farmers should get a fair and predictable price for their harvest, safe working conditions, a living wage, and the right to organize. Such a fair price will also help farming families to eat better, keep their kids in school, improve health and housing, and invest in their futures.

While the movement is market-based, it differs from "free trade," which hallows price above all. For TransFair, the certifying arm and chief cheerleader of the fair trade movement in the U.S., the goal is to empower and enrich the lives of family farmers and workers around the world.

Fair Trade is also sometime confused with organic practices. However, organic certification is concerned with how the coffee, bananas, and other products are grown and processed, whereas fair trade certification focuses upon how farmers are paid and treated. Coffee is by far the largest product sold under fair trade terms. Like all global commodities, its price fluctuates wildly and producers have no control over those gyrations.

With fair trade, farmers are guaranteed a set price of $1.26 per pound of coffee. If the world price falls below that, the farmer gets his $1.26. If it's above that, the farmer gets the same payment, plus a social premium of five cents per pound that goes to his cooperative. In return, farmers agree to certain practices such as the democratic management of the cooperative, environmentally sustainable production, public accountability, and financial transparency.

Here in the States, TransFair dreams of creating a social movement of millions of inspired conscious consumers, voting daily with their shopping dollars to lead a fundamental shift in the way food companies do business. But fair trade is not without its critics. On the right, *The Economist* magazine and others say Fair Trade is a misguided attempt to make up for market failures while encouraging inefficiencies and overproduction. On the left, some, like Professor Daniel Jaffee, author of *Brewing Justice,* worry that fair trade is merely a niche market, another flavor like hazelnut, and not a genuine global movement for social and economic change.

Fair trade is not the new millennium of world trade, I've decided. But it's a good step toward greater equity between producer and consumer. I'll drink that half a cup over no cup at all.

Textbooks or Texas-books?

Every ten years, like the census, the Texas state board of education looks at its school curriculum and decides what to revise. Since these are elected positions, it can be a highly charged process. This year the sparks flew across the nation. Through hundreds of amendments to a teacher-written draft, the 10-5 Republican majority has made a hard right turn. In a kind of intellectual spoils system, they have declared war on liberalism, secular humanism, and relativistic thinking.

They have pushed to give creationism equal standing with evolution. They have played down the role of Thomas Jefferson, because he was a deist, not a Christian. By calling the Constitution an "enduring" document, not a "living" document, they emphasize its absolutes, not its flexibility. They have replaced the term "capitalism" with that of free enterprise.

Why should we care? Isn't this just more knuckle headed-silliness in Texas? After all, one of my grade school books was titled, *The True History of the War Between the States, From the Southern Point of View.* One reason to care is that Texas is the Wal-Mart of text books. As the largest buyer of textbooks in the country, when they say "Print," the publishers only say, "How many copies?" He who controls numbers controls content. The publishers may bleat that they can tailor the text to the buyer, but in reality, they do little of that. The great seal of Texas becomes an intellectual imprimatur for books far beyond the Lone Star State.

Another reason to care is religious. As a Christian and a former high school history teacher, I don't know whether to laugh or cry. One Texas amendment asserts confidently that America was founded as a Christian nation. Across the religious-political spectrum from atheists to fundamentalist, people would agree that the Founders as a group were mostly members of Christian denominations. Indeed, the Pilgrims were one Christian sect fleeing persecution by another Christian sect. To me, such a declaration is bad theology and bad law. First, its pretense takes the Lord's name in vain. And second, it comes dangerously close to creating an UN constitutional theocracy. I'm all for teaching religion in schools. But crucially, you must insert the preposition "about."

As an example, one of the eight mega-questions in my class on Western Civilization was "How has religion been a force for great good and great evil?" That evil can come from the pathological sense of rectitude that afflicts what Eric Hoffer called "true believers." I would quote to the Texas School board words of Oliver Cromwell to the General Assembly of the Church of Scotland, "I beseech you, in the bowels of Christ, think it possible you may be mistaken."

More diplomatic are the words of Tom Ratliff, another conservative who recently defeated the most rabid member of School Board. He said, "The Board majority keeps wanting to talk about this being a Christian nation. My attitude is this country was founded by a group of men who were Christians but who didn't want the government dictating religion."

Amen.

Who Are We?

Ever since I read Edward Gibbon's *Decline And Fall Of The Roman Empire* twenty-five years ago—I confess it was only a nine hundred page abridgement—half-formed comparisons between Rome and the U.S. today have rolled around in my head like rusty pinballs. Some points on that list have been the rising income disparity and incredible conspicuous consumption, the general coarsening of society. Then there's the privatization of more and more government functions, including the military—Blackwater's outrages in Iraq come to mind. Aren't NASCAR contests just modern chariot races? Aren't NFL players just gladiators without the deaths?

Remember President Bush's exhortation after 9/11 to show our patriotism by going shopping? As Gibbon wrote, "It was artfully contrived by (the emperor) Augustus that, in the enjoyment of plenty, the Romans would lose their memory of freedom."

Now comes a new book with wit and insights that make me envious. In only 220 pages, Cullen Murphy, a former editor for *The Atlantic* magazine, answers the title's question "Are We Rome?" with a resounding "Yes, No, and Maybe."

Written as the Iraq debacle becomes clear to all who have eyes to see, Murphy relishes retelling the story of Rome's disastrous invasion of Germany when three whole legions were wiped out and when the Consul Crassus took an army to ego-driven destruction in the Iraq desert. Approvingly, he quotes my favorite theologian Reinhold Niebuhr, who said that not only were we too big for our moral britches but the larger we became, the less control we had over our own destiny.

For the pessimists, the book recounts some of the toxic mixture of arrogance and ignorance we project abroad, Washington swimming in lobbyists' money as Rome swam in corruption and our respective hypocrisies on immigration and values.

For the optimists, Murphy believes that unlike Rome we still have a reasonably functioning and responsive democracy. Our impatient national character includes willingness and an ability to change. Therefore, he says, we should stop telling others what to do and work our own political and societal salvation along these general lines:

> Seek a broader appreciation of the wider world. Rein in our unilateralist hubris and join the concert of nations.

> Stop treating government as a necessary evil, and instead support it to do the big jobs it can do well.

> Fortify the institutions that promote assimilation and build community. Among other things, that means some kind of obligatory national service.

> Take some weight off the overstretched military. As a bitter Iraqi veteran wrote in the *New York Times*, the nation's attitude has been "Party Here, Sacrifice Over There."

> Develop a long range-energy policy that pays our dues to the planet and gives us some economic moral ground to stand on.

In the course of answering, Are we Rome?, Collen Murphy elegantly and pointedly allows us to ask Who Are We?

Climate Change and Food Security

Far from Vermont's green hills and the Gulf Coast's blackening shores, far from Copenhagen's failed agreements and Congress's stalled comprehensive energy policy, I got a window on how climate change is affecting people who already have very few resources. Last month in Nicaragua I participated in a conference on finding solutions to problems of "food security". This new euphemism describes the painful zone between feast and starvation.

In particular, this situation afflicts millions of coffee farmers and their families during the so-called *mesos flacos*, or "thin months," when their one-time annual payment for coffee runs out. The conference was co-sponsored by two coffee companies, one of them Green Mountain Coffee Roasters. The goal was to train trainers to go back to their communities and teach several means to supplement their coffee income. The four options were family gardens, organic composting, edible mushrooms, and beekeeping—my specialty. Looming over all our work was a fear about the warming of the planet.

Anecdotal evidence was profuse. Farmers and extension agents pointed out the pests that are moving up in altitude where the better coffee is grown. They described changes in bean and corn cycles and the early flowering of coffee plants. The Center for Sustainable Agriculture showed stark computer models and aerial maps that marked the temperature rising across Nicaragua, the second poorest country in Latin America. Coffee is Nicaragua's chief crop and export revenue earner. In the next forty years, the areas available to grow coffee will shrink by 80 percent.

A political activist from Colombia excoriated the industrial powers, especially the United States and China, for their selfish, reckless refusal to limit carbon emissions. Santiago Dolmus, the technical director for a coffee cooperative with twenty-seven hundred farmer-family members, took a different tack. In a low but insistent voice, he urged the audience to "Take hold of your fear of climate change, don't be paralyzed. There is a lot to do. Don't extend coffee into protected forested lands," he said. "Diversify into other crops like honey, cocoa, small livestock. Develop more local foods."

He urged the farmers to reduce their slash and burn tactics, to conserve water. He called for a change in banking practices—alternative credit for alternative products. Finally, he urged a change in social attitudes. "We've got to get more men involved in these programs. The women already get it!"

Rick Peyser, the director of Social Advocacy & Coffee Community Outreach, was pleased with the results. And at the end of the four days, a number of farmers provided me with strong unsolicited testimonials about the power and value of this hands-on training. For my own part, I wished that they could have at least acknowledged the nine hundred pound gorilla of population "looming over us all" in the room. But that was not to be. When I raised the question over dinner, the reactions ranged from hostility to indifference. I suppose that's a topic for another conference and another commentary.

CPSIA information can be obtained at www.ICGtesting.com
Printed in the USA
BVOW030751271011

274612BV00005B/18/P

9 781935 922070